C000001650

WORDS OF COMFORT IN TIMES OF GRIEF

# Scent
*of*
# Water

## PENELOPE
## SWITHINBANK

Sarah
GRACE
PUBLISHING
**Dyslexic Friendly**

First published 2021 by Sarah Grace Publishing
an imprint of Malcolm Down Publishing ltd.
www.sarahgracepublishing.co.uk

24 23 22 21    7 6 5 4 3 2 1

The right of Penelope Swithinbank to be identified as the author of this work has been asserted by her in accordance with the Copyright, Designs and Patents Act 1988.

All rights reserved. No part of this publication may be reproduced, stored in a retrieval system, or transmitted in any other form or by any means, electronic, mechanical, photocopying, recording or otherwise, without the prior permission of the publisher.

British Library Cataloguing in Publication Data
A catalogue record for this book is available from the British Library.

ISBN 978-1-912863-73-0

Scripture quotations marked NIV are taken from
New International Version (Anglicised edition)
Copyright ©1979, 1984, 2011 by Biblica (formerly International Bible Society). Used by permission of Hodder & Stoughton Publishers, an Hachette UK company. All rights reserved. 'NIV' is a registered trademark of Biblica (formerly International Bible Society). UK trademark number 1448790.

Scripture quotations marked MSG are taken from The Message
Copyright © 1993, 2002, 2018 by Eugene H. Peterson

Scripture quotations marked NLT are taken from Holy Bible, New Living Translation, copyright © 1996, 2004, 2015 by Tyndale House Foundation. Used by permission of Tyndale House Publishers, Inc., Carol Stream, Illinois 60188. All rights reserved.

Scripture quotations marked ISV are taken from International Standard Version Copyright © 1995-2014 by ISV Foundation. ALL RIGHTS RESERVED INTERNATIONALLY. Used by permission of Davidson Press, LLC.

Scripture quotations marked AMP are taken from Amplified Bible (Copyright © 2015 by The Lockman Foundation, La Habra, CA 90631. All rights reserved.

Scripture quotations marked AMP Classic Edition are taken from Amplified Bible, Classic Edition (AMPC)
Copyright © 1954, 1958, 1962, 1964, 1965, 1987 by The Lockman Foundation

Scripture quotations marked KJV are taken from King James Version

Scripture quotations marked NRSV are taken from New Revised Standard Version Bible, copyright © 1989 the Division of Christian Education of the National Council of the Churches of Christ in the United States of America. Used by permission. All rights reserved.

Scripture quotations marked Douay-Rheims are taken from Douay-Rheims 1899 American Edition

Scripture quotations marked NASB are taken from New American Standard Bible (NASB) New American Standard Bible®, Copyright © 1960, 1971, 1977, 1995, 2020 by The Lockman Foundation. All rights reserved.

Scripture quotations marked GWT are taken from GOD'S WORD Translation Copyright © 1995, 2003, 2013, 2014, 2019, 2020 by God's Word to the Nations Mission Society. All rights reserved.

Scripture quotations marked ESV are taken from ESV UK The Holy Bible, English Standard Version Copyright © 2001 by Crossway Bibles, a division of Good News Publishers.

Scripture quotations marked NCV are taken from The Holy Bible, New Century Version®. Copyright © 2005 by Thomas Nelson, Inc.

Scripture quotations marked RSV are taken from Revised Standard Version of the Bible, copyright © 1946, 1952, and 1971 the Division of Christian Education of the National Council of the Churches of Christ in the United States of America. Used by permission. All rights reserved.

Scripture quotations marked TPT are taken from The Passion Translation®. Copyright © 2017 by BroadStreet Publishing® Group, LLC. Used by permission. All rights reserved. thePassionTranslation.com

Scripture quotations marked Darby are taken from Darby Translation

Scripture quotations marked HCSB are taken from Holman Christian Standard Bible (HCSB) Copyright © 1999, 2000, 2002, 2003, 2009 by Holman Bible Publishers, Nashville Tennessee. All rights reserved.

Scripture quotations marked ASV are taken from American Standard Version

Geneva Bible, 1599 Edition. Published by Tolle Lege Press

Photographs by Revd Canon Debbie Dewes
Cover design by Angela Selfe
Art direction by Sarah Grace

Printed in the UK by Bell and Bain Ltd, Glasgow

*In memory of my mother*

**Irene M. Walter**
(neé Lanston)

22.01.20 – 23.09.10

Giving thanks to God
for her life, love, and prayers

*Charm is deceptive,*
*and beauty does not last;*
*but a woman who fears the LORD*
*will be greatly praised.*
Proverbs 31:30 (NLT)

**There is hope for a tree
when it is cut down.
. . . merely a scent of water
will make it sprout . . .**

*Job 14:7-9 (GWT)*

# Contents

Introduction     11

Notes of Explanation     15

A Week of Extra Special Days     17

## DEVOTIONS

Immanuel, God with Us: even in loneliness     29

Punched in the Stomach: shock and agony     35

The Brook Besor: allowing myself to rest     39

Concerning the Morning Aid: when God seems far away     45

From a Deep Hole: when I can't see the light     51

Busy Thoughts: of fear, disappointment, hope     57

The Waters of Grief: causing fear of drowning     63

Close to Me: together in Christ     69

What of Those Who Die Without Christ?     73

Psalm 23: unruly emotions     75

The Lord Cares Deeply: when his loved ones die     81

Praying for Those Who Have Died     87

The Communion of Saints: surrounded by a great cloud of witnesses     93

Walking Through the Valley: three months of grief     99

Peace: which passes all understanding     105

God's Arms: wanting to know God's help     109

Where is God When it Hurts: the God who sees     113

Raging Seas: overwhelmed by grief     117

Melted in His Sunlove: frozen with grief                               123

Learning to Lean: when I need to rest                                  127

The Hand of God: does God allow (or even cause) pain?                  133

El Shaddai: wanting to know that God is all-sufficient                 139

A New Day Dawning: a daily remembering                                 143

All – Always: is God really able?                                      149

Going Forward: giving thanks in the brokenness                         153

## REFLECTIONS for dipping into

Oaks of Righteousness                                                  163

The Gossamer Web                                                       165

The Promise of Peace                                                   167

Time for Something New                                                 169

One Thing                                                              171

Why Me?                                                                173

An Invitation                                                          177

The Fellowship of the Mat                                              179

Learning to Live Without                                               181

Snowdrops                                                              183

Between Walls                                                          185

The Last Battle                                                        187

Acknowledgements                                                       189

Further Help                                                           191

Notes                                                                  193

Our loved ones are with him.
He is with us.
Together in him.
They are very near.

# Introduction

Today – the day I'm writing this – is my mother's birthday. She would be celebrating her 100th birthday this year and would be overjoyed to celebrate with her family around her: two daughters, five grandchildren, six great-grandchildren. She met four of the great-grandchildren and adored them.

This year, too, is another decade anniversary: ten years since my mother died in an accident. She drove me to the station for my train – yes, she was still driving, still very active at ninety. We'd had a wonderful 90th birthday party for her, and at the end everyone said, 'See you in ten years for her next big celebration!' There was nothing to indicate she wouldn't live another decade. Her mother, my grandmother, was nearly ninety-nine when she suddenly decided one night it was time to 'Go Home', as she cheerfully put it, and died in her sleep. Longevity is in my maternal family line.

My mother died tragically and suddenly as I watched the out-of-control car sweep her away. Afterwards, as I plunged into deep depression, I found nothing that reached my dark soul of the night, nothing that helped me know that God was still with me. I was numbed by grief, frozen into solitude and nothing and no one seemed to be able to penetrate my protective walls. I found it very difficult to pray or to read the Bible. I couldn't concentrate, nothing seemed to help, and I wished there was a specific daily devotional to help me to connect with the Lord in and through the grief.

For a full two years I was there. At times I barely clung on. When hugs rubbed me raw and consoling, well-meant clichés did not ring true. When God seemed far away. I was far away. I couldn't read. Anything, let alone the Bible. When the depression and the blackness were all-consuming and life was barely worth living.

Eventually, out of that experience, I wrote a daily devotional to help others going through the first six months of bereavement. Those who found it on my website and either used it themselves, or passed it on to others who were grieving the loss of a loved one, kept asking me to publish it so that it could be easily given to those who mourn. Maybe as a gift in their time of need.

So here is *Scent of Water*. I'm hoping it will help others in times of bereavement and grief. Just a verse and a few thoughts for the times when mourning and grief mean that anything longer, anything deeper, is impossible.

For those days when finger-tip-hanging is by a single nail.

When grief is all-consuming, raw, inconsolable.

The days when it is a raging torrent, a swirling river, a catastrophic tsunami. And the days when it seems only a brook, a stream, a trickle and you know it's just waiting to roar on again. The days when the waters of grief are lapping at your toes; or your tears become a waterfall.

And now I offer it to you, whose heart is broken, whose heart has a hole the shape of a loved one who is no longer with you. May the Lord meet with you on and through this sob-wracked pathway, binding up the broken-hearted.

I am aware that grief and mourning live differently with different people. Some experience tears and sobs, heartache and darkness.

Others feel numbness, disbelief, anger, guilt. Or a mixture of all that and more.

We each have our own pathway to walk through the 'valley of the shadow of death' (Psalm 23:4, AMP). We each mourn in our own way, and even that can vary, depending on our relationship with the one who has died.

This ten-year anniversary seems a fitting time to publish *Scent of Water* as a celebration of a life well-lived by a woman who loved the Lord, who had an enormous gift of faithful prayer, who was loved by so many, and especially by her family. Who would have been humbly glad if her death could be a source of inspiration to help others draw closer to her Lord Jesus.

My mother, Irene Walter. I am extraordinarily and deeply grateful to have known and been loved by such a wonderful woman.

And I pray that this Scent of Water which came from the ending of her life will help you, the ones who mourn, to know that you are deeply loved by the God who walks this painful path with you. And that it's OK to grieve, because grief is the price we pay for love. Perhaps the greater the love we have for the one who has died, the greater the grief when we mourn them, and therefore the greater the honour we pay them by our grief.

Let my grief be a reminder to me of how much I loved and was loved, and a reminder to be grateful for that love.

Love never dies. It is stronger than death *(see Song of Songs 8:6).*

Penelope Swithinbank

All praise to the God and Father of our Master, Jesus the Messiah! Father of all mercy! God of all healing counsel! He comes alongside us when we go through hard times, and before you know it, he brings alongside someone else who is going through hard times so that we can be there for that person just as God was there for us. We have plenty of hard times that come from following the Messiah, but no more so than the good times of his healing comfort – we get a full measure of that, too.

*2 Corinthians 1:3-5 (MSG)*

# Notes of Explanation

Sometimes in the comments there is a line ___

It is a blank space where you can whisper the name of the one for whom you grieve.

**The weeks don't have to be read in the order they are given here**. They have a theme or topic title, so that you can choose what's most helpful for that day. Sometimes it may be helpful to flick through and allow your eyes to alight on something that seems relevant or helpful for today, for this week. You can dip in and out, follow through in the published order, or choose your own way of using the book. Whatever's most helpful for you for now.

There are 25 weeks, each of which are for Monday–Saturday, as there's probably church on Sunday. There's a section for special days – the funeral, the first Christmas, anniversaries, birthdays. At the end are some reflections and meditations, with accompanying photos, to be read once or many times, whatever's helpful.

You don't have to read every day. Yet this may well be the scent of water your soul craves. Even just a few moments might help you to know the love of the God who walks alongside you and loves you in and through your grief, your tears. Maybe there are sometimes things that we only see through our tears, things that when dry-eyed, are invisible.

May you see, may you know, that this is the chance for God to put his arms around you and hold you in his love in ways you had never even imagined.

# A Week of Extra Special Days
## Thankfulness

Some days during the first months of mourning are so important, so shattering, so huge in their grief, that they require something special.

Everyone's grief is so different, and I only know mine. But I also know that learning to find gratitude in the grief and brokenness is an important part of the journey.

Remembering to be grateful even for the smallest of things makes an enormous difference! Do it as you go; or as you slip into bed at night. What were the good things, where did God bless you, where did you find the tiniest joy today?

The song of the birds, a card from a friend, the aroma of coffee, a bubble bath . . . Making a list and learning to be grateful even in the brokenness. Learning to feel joy even when faced with disappointment and despair. Choosing to 'give thanks in all circumstances' (1 Thessalonians 5:18, NIV). Even in the brokenness and grief.

Each grief is unique; the only way to go is through it. Learning to adjust to a 'new normal' can be hard, makes you feel crazy, as your feelings bounce around and refuse to follow the prescribed stages of the experts! Society often assumes we should just get on with it, hide our tears in public and bury the grief. That only makes us feel guilty when we are unable to control our emotions and it makes us push them down rather than facing them, going through them, and accepting the loss as part of the price we pay for love in our lives.

# The Day of the Funeral

My heart is frozen. I can't believe this day has come. Some people's tears become a raging torrent or a flooded waterfall; for others it's like ice. It's hard to hear above the sound of the waters. Or through the ice. It's impossible for me to reach out or for me to feel others reaching out to me. But today, today, I want to be strong, Lord.

There'll be others grieving at this service, others missing ____ .

I commit this day of all days to you, Lord God. Help me to give thanks for ____'s life and for all the love we shared and knew.

Give me the strength I need today, Lord. The courage to stand straight and acknowledge my pain, even when the tears flow. The ability to comfort others with the comfort you are giving me. The peace that only you can give.

And especially, the ability to remember that you're faithful and be thankful.

Jesus promised:

**'I will not leave you as orphans [comfortless, desolate, bereaved, and helpless]; I will come [back] to you.'**

*John 14:18 (AMP)*

*May I know your presence with me.*
*Today and always.*

# The Day After the Funeral

Nothingness. Emptiness.

___ is gone, and nothing can bring them back. I'm going through the motions – or not – automatically, frozenly, numbly. I still can't believe this is the start of life without them.

Yesterday was like the end of an era; almost an end of me too. Others were wanting to be hugged and to hug me. It felt like my raw wounds being rubbed; it was agony.

Yet you, Lord God, are in it all with me. I have to believe that. I don't feel blessed in any sense whatsoever, so hold me, Lord. Hold me close. I've nothing else except you.

**You're blessed when you're at the end of your rope. With less of you there is more of God and his rule.**

**You're blessed when you feel you've lost what is most dear to you. Only then can you be embraced by the One most dear to you.**

*Matthew 5:3-4 (MSG)*

*I need to know your embrace today, Lord.*

# Christmas

Christmas won't be the same without ____

Ever. Or so it seems right now.

There'll be a ____ shaped emptiness around the table, singing carols, by the tree, opening presents. It's times like these I really miss ____ . But I don't want to mope, to spoil the day for the rest of the family, friends, other people.

I know I will be wobbly inside, tears will be near, the ache will be more pronounced. But today is about YOU, Jesus, and your coming to earth. Fill me with the love of the Christ child today, Lord; thank you for being my Counsellor, my Almighty God, my Everlasting Father, my Prince of Peace[1] – my all in all.

> **The people who walked in darkness**
> **have seen a great light.**
> **For those who lived in a land of deep shadows –**
> **light! . . .**
> **For a child has been born – for us!**
> **the gift of a son – for us!**
> **He'll take over**
> **the running of the world.**
> **His names will be: Amazing Counselor,**
> **Strong God,**
> **Eternal Father,**
> **Prince of Wholeness.**
>
> *Isaiah 9:2,6 (MSG)*

*May I see your light today in spite of the darkness inside me. Immanuel: God is with me.*

# New Year

What a strange feeling – that it all happened last year, that I won't see ____ this year at all.

'Last year' makes their going all the more distant. It's last year since we hugged, last year we talked. I'm going into this new year knowing I won't see them, hear them, this year.

The normal anticipation of a new year, with its connotations of new beginnings and fresh starts, of opportunities and events, is tinged with sadness, sorrow, aloneness.

Yet I *don't* go into it alone. You, Lord, are by my side, the God who makes all things new. You promised to be with me; I claim that promise now, Lord, as I step over the threshold of this new year. Keep me by your side.

**Be sure of this: I am with you always, even to the end of the age.**

*Matthew 28:20 (NLT)*

*Be with me today, Lord God. And throughout the whole of this new year.*

# Their Birthday

I know I don't have to do anything special today – there is no 'should' about it all. And maybe no one else will really notice anything different about today. But because it's a birthday, the sorrow washes over me anew. The alone-ness is intensified.

The memories of other birthdays crowd in. I feel as if I've been through the wringer – head-achey, eyes sore and red-rimmed, sorrow starting up again and surprising me by its intensity.

Birthdays should be happy occasions, a time for celebrating. And through the fog of my grief, I want to celebrate, to be grateful for memories of happier birthdays.

Joy and sorrow and love, all bound up together, on this birthday.

**Every good and perfect gift is from above, coming down from the Father of the heavenly lights, who does not change like shifting shadows. He chose to give us birth through the word of truth, that we might be a kind of firstfruits of all he created.**

*James 1:17-18 (NIV)*

*Thank you, Lord, for the gift of ___ . Thank you for the memories of happy birthdays and celebrations. Thank you for all the years we had together. Thank you for all your good gifts.*

# My Birthday

There's no card or present from ___ of course. True, others have remembered my birthday and I am glad and grateful. But still, I miss that one phone call, card, voice; I'm noticing the absence, yet in the absence I can be grateful for all the years, all the memories, all the times we *were* together on this day.

> **For you created . . . me . . . I praise you because I am fearfully and wonderfully made . . .**
>
> *Psalm 139:13-14 (NIV)*

> **He will take delight in you with gladness. . . . He will rejoice over you with joyful songs.**
>
> *Zephaniah 3:17 (NLT)*

*I'm thankful that you know me, created me, give me another year. Thank you, Lord, for rejoicing over me and making me ME!*

# Wedding Anniversary

Today would have been – no, IS – our wedding anniversary. And I am here alone.

One half of a whole. It feels like a part of me is missing; we were two become one (Ephesians 5:31) and half of me is gone.

I miss ___ more than I ever felt possible. But today of all days, I want to give thanks for the life we had together, for all we shared: the good and the bad. I long for ___'s touch, hug, kiss.

Grief is the price I am paying for love. I hate being the one left behind.

**Many waters cannot quench love; rivers cannot wash it away.**
*Song of Songs 8:7 (NIV)*

*As I mourn again today, Lord, remind me of all the wonderful times we had, of all that we meant to one another. Forgive me for not saying 'I love you' enough, forgive me for all the times I shouted, stormed, turned away. Lord, take away the painful memories and keep me thankful for the good ones. I want to notice and remember and be grateful for all the happy times.*

# One Year to the Day

I've been on a long hard journey this past year. I can scarcely believe it is only one year! In some ways it feels like yesterday since ___ died, in other ways it feels like a lifetime ago. I'm learning to live with this 'new normal.' It's not been easy and I've still some way to go; I can appreciate why people used to wear mourning clothes for two years.

But I know there comes an end to this grieving; that I carry ___ in my heart forever and I know s/he would not want me to put my life on hold for much longer. I'm learning, just beginning to learn, to live **with** this new normal.

I know that one day, one day, death will be gone for good, that the Lord will 'wipe away all tears' (Revelation 21:4, KJV), and we will be with him without pain or sorrow or grief.

**I heard a voice thunder from the Throne: 'Look! Look! God has moved into the neighborhood, making his home with men and women! They're his people, he's their God. He'll wipe every tear from their eyes. Death is gone for good – tears gone, crying gone, pain gone – all the first order of things gone.' The Enthroned continued, 'Look! I'm making everything new. Write it all down – each word dependable and accurate.'**

**_Revelation 21:3-5 (MSG)_**

_I'm not sure where this year has gone, Lord Jesus. Some days I've been very aware of you walking with me in the sorrow, other days you've seemed far away. I'm still learning to walk this path of bereavement. Hold my hand and wipe away my tears._

# Devotions

# IMMANUEL, GOD WITH US

## even in loneliness

*Grief can be a solitary and isolating experience for many of us. Jesus knew the depth of grief like that. This week's readings help us to realise that he knows, he understands, he is there IN it with us.*

### MONDAY

**He was . . . a man of sorrows, acquainted with deepest grief.**
**. . . it was our sorrows that weighed him down.**
*Isaiah 53:3-4 (NLT)*

Jesus knew grief; the sense of the words in Hebrew is that he was familiar with deepest calamity and sorrow. He knew; he knows. And he carries my sorrows. They were part of his grief!

I don't even have to tell him – he knows how I'm feeling today. He knows, he carries, he cares.

*Thank you, Lord, for knowing. Thank you for carrying my sorrow.*

### TUESDAY

**Jesus burst into tears.**          *John 11:35 (ISV)*

These words give me permission to grieve. Not that I need it – although sometimes in our Western culture I feel I do need that permission! Too many times I've been told that it's all for the best; that they are in a better place.

They may be, but I am left here without them, and I hurt. My tears fall unchecked and I want to hide. Public grief is not always easy for some of us.

But it was for Jesus; he burst into tears as he arrived at the tomb of his close friend Lazarus. He was not ashamed of his grief. Death causes tears.

*Lord, all I can give you today are my tears. Thank you for crying with me.*

## WEDNESDAY

**For we do not have a high priest who is unable to sympathize with our weaknesses . . .**

*Hebrews 4:15 (NRSV)*

Jesus understands not just the facts of my grief, he understands the feelings too. He understands the pain, the depression, the anger, the hurt of being left alone. Far from being cold and heartless, he's full of tenderness and sympathy. He too knows the full gamut of emotions. Even if those around me try to understand, how can they know just how I'm feeling today? Bless them for trying; but I feel that they can't know exactly how it is for me right now.

And if I seem unable to let tears fall, I know I need to express my grief in other ways today. What might help me to do that – shall I paint or write or exercise hard?

*Lord, you truly **do** know, and you truly **do** understand. You have experienced every single emotion. Only you can fully sympathise. Let me know your feelings in this with me today. And be with me as I express my grief in my own way.*

## THURSDAY

**They will call him Immanuel (which means 'God with us').**
*Matthew 1:23 (NIV)*

God-with-us, you are in this with me. You know how it is; you know I have to go through this path of grief. But you are here in it **with me!** And I am so glad I don't have to go through it alone. Thank you, thank you!

Sometimes my grief feels like fear; when you're with me, Lord, I needn't fear this torrent of sadness.

*Keep close to me, Lord, otherwise I fear I won't get through today. Just saying your name, Immanuel, means a great deal to me today. Immanuel. God with me. Today.*

## FRIDAY

**Let us come boldly to the throne of our gracious God. There we will receive his mercy, and we will find grace to help us when we need it most.**
*Hebrews 4:16 (NLT)*

I'm learning again that it's not a failure to come to the throne of grace; it isn't a sign of weakness or something wrong with me! Nor that I'm not spiritual if I have this depression, this huge sense of grief or anger. I'm learning this is a normal part of being human and alive. God, you welcome me to come to you.

At the throne of grace there is help when I need it most – your love and mercy and pure grace are there, ready to be poured out over me. Every day. Whenever I need it. Today.

*Grace to help. I need Your grace today, Lord. I come boldly, tearfully, to your throne and receive and accept your grace.*

## SATURDAY

**He told them, 'My soul is crushed with grief to the point of death.'**

*Matthew 26:38 (NLT)*

Lord Jesus, it cost you a lot, everything, to walk the path of suffering and death. You experienced the deepest feelings, emotions and pain.

Experienced them to the point of being so crushed, so depressed, that life itself seemed almost pointless. In the depth of my own sorrow, I am yet again amazed that you could reach this point – could know, could truly know, just how it is.

*Hallelujah, what a Saviour! Thank you that I don't need to panic, because you are with me and you are my God (see Isaiah 41:10, MSG).*

# PUNCHED IN THE STOMACH

## shock and agony

King David probably wrote Psalm 142, when he was afraid of his enemies and hiding in a cave. That's all I want to do right now – to hide, curl up in the enveloping darkness, sleep away this time.

But I need to learn to copy David – to bring all my troubles to the Lord, to look up at God, knowing he will bring me out of this dark place, knowing I need to praise him, even in this horrendous time.

*Being grateful in the brokenness.*

### MONDAY

**I cry out to the LORD; I plead for the LORD's mercy.**

*Psalm 142:1 (NLT)*

This grief, this unexpected grief (for death and bereavement are always unexpected, even after a long illness) – it feels as if I have been punched in the stomach. My internal muscles clench with the shock and the agony of it all. I feel nauseous. All I can do – and what better thing to do is there? – all I can do is cry out to the Lord.

*Lord, save me from this agony!*

## TUESDAY

**I spill out all my complaints before him, and spell out my troubles in detail . . .**

*Psalm 142:2 (MSG)*

Throughout a sleepless night, tears coming and going, deep sobs racking me through and through, I pour out what I feel (or don't feel) to God. It spills out of me as I cry out to him.

*Lord, save me from this agony.*

## WEDNESDAY

**When I am overwhelmed, you alone know the way I should turn.**

*Psalm 142:3 (NLT)*

I can barely hold on; it is so overwhelming. But my trust is in you, God. You are my strength, my love, my fortress, my strong tower. There is no one else who knows me, knows what I should do.

*Lord, save me from this agony.*

## THURSDAY

**I look for someone to come and help me, but no one gives me a passing thought! No one will help me; no one cares a bit what happens to me.**

*Psalm 142:4 (NLT)*

I know there are people I might talk to – friends or family; but never have I felt so *ALONE*. Not lonely – although that too, sometimes –

but this aloneness, this being estranged from normality, makes me feel as if there is no one who really understands. But you do, my Lord and my God.

*Lord, save me from this agony.*

## FRIDAY

**Then I pray to you, O LORD. I say, 'You are my place of refuge. You are all I really want in life. Hear my cry, for I am very low.'**
**Psalm 142: 5-6 (NLT)**

Oh, am I low! Very low. Sometimes I feel I'm in a deep hole. I am plumbing the depths but I know you are deeper than my deepest hole, dear God.

*Lord, save me from this agony.*

## SATURDAY

**Bring me out of prison so I can thank you . . . for you are good to me.**
**Psalm 142:7 (NLT)**

You alone, Lord, can bring healing and comfort and security. Even in the depths I can look for things to be thankful for, little gifts from you that turn my burden into blessings.
Today I thank you for – and for – and for –
(Small things, like the smell of coffee, the bright sun, a comfy bed, that note from a friend . . .)

*Lord, thank you that you will save me from this agony.*

# THE BROOK BESOR

## allowing myself to rest

This week's daily thoughts are based on the story of King David and his men in 1 Samuel 30. They've been away fighting the Philistines and return home to Ziklag only to discover it's been sacked. They've lost everything – their homes destroyed and their families taken away. They're devastated. David urges them to pick themselves up, get going again and rescue their families. But some of the soldiers are too tired, and unable to move. David tells them to stay and rest by the Brook Besor. Later, when he and the army return victorious with the families AND the spoils of war, David insists that those who'd had to rest still receive their shares of everything. Sometimes it's good to have permission to rest.

### MONDAY

**David and his men wept aloud until they had no strength left to weep.**

*1 Samuel 30:4 (NIV)*

David and his men have the normal reaction to grief – tears rain down until exhaustion hits. My tears are a reminder to me of how much I loved and was loved, and a reminder to be grateful for that love.

*These men wept together. Lord, I need someone to weep with me today. Will you weep with me?*

## TUESDAY

**But David found strength in the LORD his God.**

*1 Samuel 30:6 (NIV)*

Confronted with disaster, bereft and lonely, David did the only thing he could: he went to the Lord. He'd lost his wife and children, his companions were blaming him for the disaster, and he felt totally alone and misunderstood.

*Lord, that's how I feel: alone and devastated by my grief. Please strengthen me today.*

## WEDNESDAY

**Then David said to Abiathar the priest . . .**

*1 Samuel 30:7 (NIV)*

After resting in the Lord, David turned to a friend – he called on his pastor for spiritual advice. Sometimes talking with a trusted friend or with a wise pastor can help to ease and to understand the grief.

*Lord, show me who I should turn to. And when. Actually – please just send someone, nudge the right person into coming to me.*

## THURSDAY

**Then David asked the LORD . . .**                 *1 Samuel 30:8 (NLT)*

What shall I do, Lord? I feel lost, overcome and cheated. Yes, cheated! I feel cheated that I'm not going to know her/him grow older. I feel cheated that s/he isn't going to enjoy a much longer life. Now I am consumed by all that I am feeling today.

*So I'm asking you, Lord, just like David did. Guide me, show me, help me.*
    *And keep me in touch with you.*

## FRIDAY

**They came to the torrent Besor: and some being weary stayed there.**

*1 Samuel 30:9 (DRA)*

Resting by the brook, too weary to go any further, worn out by grief. Allowed to stay, allowed to rest, allowed time to recover.
    I too am resting at the Brook Besor, needing time to recover. And that's OK; I don't have to do what I would normally do. I can have this time out for now. And that's such a relief to know.

*Thank you, Lord, for rest and refreshment. For unlimited time at the Brook Besor.*

## SATURDAY

**We share and share alike – those who go to battle and those who guard the equipment.**

*1 Samuel 30:24 (NLT)*

It's not a disgrace to have this time out. This is one of those times when I need to stay by the Brook Besor. David was generous to those who had stayed, exhausted and worn out; he treated them the same as those who'd continued into battle.

God's grace is a generous grace. HE understands, even if others don't seem to.

*Lord, thank you for allowing me this time at the Brook Besor. Thank you for undeserved grace.*

# CONCERNING THE MORNING AID

## when God seems far away

How did Jesus cope with pain, sorrow and isolation? He quoted words from Psalm 22 when he was on the cross, and it's a good psalm for this week's readings. The title given to this psalm in the Septuagint translation (the LXX) is 'Concerning the Morning Aid' and so there is a play on words here – 'morning aid' sounds like 'mourning aid.'

### MONDAY

**Concerning the Morning Aid**                    *Psalm 22 (LXX title)*

Maybe I can't read all of this poetical, deeply painful psalm right now; not yet. But I know Jesus knew it, for he shouted words from it while in immense, intense agony on the cross. Sorrow and suffering, aloneness and unansweredness. Counting my bones, for I am unable to eat.

But into the dark night of my soul, into my sadness, comes this word: the morning aid. Say it aloud and it becomes my mourning aid. I start today knowing that HE is my mourning aid. My aid this morning.

*Lord Jesus, you understand, and you know what I need right now. Please be my mourning aid today.*

## TUESDAY

**My God, my God, why have you abandoned me? Why are you so far away when I groan for help?**

*Psalm 22:1 (NLT)*

Lord God, it does seem at times as though you are far, far away. I can't feel your nearness; I can't feel very much at all, actually. My heart is frozen. Sorrow for now is all-consuming. I am groaning – 'roaring,' as one translation[2] says.

The funeral was so – final. Life for others has returned to normal. But I am bereft, struggling to find my new normal.

*Help me to know that you haven't abandoned me; that your love still surrounds me. Even in this.*

## WEDNESDAY

**Every day I call to you, my God, but you do not answer. Every night I lift my voice, but I find no relief.**

*Psalm 22:2 (NLT)*

I know that God hears me – but I can't hear his words to me. I am sleepless, tossing and turning, thinking and remembering. Help me to remember more of the happy times, God, more of the good things. Thank you for the times we enjoyed. I'm sorry I didn't say, 'I love you' more often. But I did love, do love and that's why I'm feeling much grief. It's the cost of love.

*Hear my voice today, Lord God. And let me hear you whispering back to me.*

## THURSDAY

**Yet you are holy, enthroned on the praises of Israel. Our ancestors trusted in you, and you rescued them. They cried out to you and were saved. . . . In You they trusted and were not disappointed.**

*Psalm 22:3-5 (NLT); 5 (NASB)*

I've known that too, Lord – in difficulties and hard times you've been there for me in the past, so I know I can trust you now. Even though it doesn't feel like it, I know that you care, that you are with me in this.

*Thank you for your unending love and faithfulness. I know this in my head; I just wish I could feel you more right now. Let me hear you speaking; help me to trust you. Don't let me be disappointed!*

## FRIDAY

**My strength has dried up like sunbaked clay. My tongue sticks to the roof of my mouth.**

*Psalm 22:15 (NLT)*

Grieving is tiring. Everything feels exhausting right now, but my grief saps my strength. I've very little reserve energy, and things I normally do without a thought now seem to take a huge effort to accomplish.

Heavenly Father, I think you're telling me that this is all right, that this is normal. To go slowly – to rest, to be content to achieve less than I normally do – is good for this time.

I remember that I can rest by the Brook Besor.

*O Lord, do not stay far away! You are my strength; come quickly to my aid!*

Psalm 22:19 (NLT)

## SATURDAY

**All who seek the LORD will praise him. Their hearts will rejoice with everlasting joy.**

*Psalm 22:26 (NLT)*

I know that God will grant an end to this sorrow one day. That one day I'll know his love and comfort in all their realities. Not that I will stop missing ___ but that I'll no longer be consumed by the overwhelming grief I'm experiencing right now.

He will come, as my mourning aid. He will come – he does come.

*His coming is as certain as the morning.*
Hosea 6:3 (translated from an old French version)

*Come, Lord Jesus, come to my aid and help me to praise and rejoice in you, even from the depths of my grief!*

In our days of weakness, O Christ, let us trust in your strength; in our hours of darkness let us see your light; in our seasons of doubt let us feel your presence; and in our moments of despair let us cling to your cross. Amen.

*François Fénelon* (1651-1715)

# FROM A DEEP HOLE

## when I can't see the light

Grief can sometimes feel like a heavy burden that has to be carried. It saps our strength, causing weakness and weariness. **But God** – don't you love those words? – but 'God is our refuge and strength' (Psalm 46:1, NIV) as Isaiah must have known. These words from Isaiah 40 help in the daily need for the Lord's support.

### MONDAY

**Why do you complain, Jacob . . . [and] say, Israel, 'My way is hidden from the LORD; my cause is disregarded by my God'?**

*Isaiah 40:27 (NIV)*

Why do I say? Because sometimes it's how I feel – that 'my cause is disregarded by my God.' Because sometimes my grief and loneliness are overpowering and I can't seem to find the comfort God's given me in other times, in other situations.

Yet it's strangely comforting to know that others have felt like that before. They too said that God seemed almost uninterested in their situation. I'm not the only one thinking that.

*Help me to know more surely today that you are with me, supporting me, caring for me, my God.*

## TUESDAY

**Do you not know? Have you not heard? The LORD is the everlasting God, the Creator of the ends of the earth.**

*Isaiah 40:28 (NIV)*

Yes, I know you created the world, Lord God, and that you can do anything. That if you were able to create the world and everything in it, including me, then you're able to strengthen me. My confidence must be in you.

It's a very small amount of confidence and it wavers occasionally and even falters sometimes. But I trust in you, even in and through this 'valley of the shadow of death' (Psalm 23:4, AMP).

*And I know you are with me. Thank you for being there.*

## WEDNESDAY

**He never grows weak or weary. No one can measure the depths of his understanding.**

*Isaiah 40:28 (NLT)*

You are the everlasting God and you never change. Your strength goes on forever. As does your understanding. Some days I feel as if I am in a really deep, dark hole. But you are deeper still, Lord God, and underneath are your 'everlasting arms' (Deuteronomy 33:27, NIV).

*Hold me, Lord; hold me. In the depths of my despair, hold me close to you.*

## THURSDAY

**He gives strength to those who grow tired and increases the strength of those who are weak.**

*Isaiah 40:29 (GWT)*

This grief of mine is heavy and tiring as I carry it around all the time. But I'm not ready to put it down, not yet. I hug it to me, finding strange comfort in the carrying of it.

And I'm strengthened by the One who understands, who knows me and knows my burden, and who gives me strength.

*Lord, I need that strength today. Your strength, because mine has evaporated!*

## FRIDAY

**But those who trust in the LORD will find new strength. They will soar high on wings like eagles.**

*Isaiah 40:31 (NLT)*

Trust – waiting, hoping, putting my confidence in the Lord. I *have* to rely on you, Lord – I can't do this in my own strength. One day, I'll be able to soar like an eagle, with joy and freedom; but for now, all I can do is simply and only trust in you.

*I can say it; but Lord, help me to do it. Keep me trusting in you.*

## SATURDAY

**They will run and not grow weary. They will walk and not faint.**

*Isaiah 40:31 (NLT)*

I can't remember how that felt – the running and not growing weary. And I'm not sure I actually want to be like that right now. But it's comforting to know that one day, one day, I will be strong again in the strength that God gives.

*Thank you, Lord, for your faithfulness, your comfort, your strength. And thank you that your strength never ends. It's always there for me.*

# BUSY THOUGHTS

## of fear, disappointment, hurt

Psalm 94 is about things that fill our thoughts. Troubled thoughts, disappointed thoughts, perplexing thoughts, sad thoughts. All the 'whys' and 'where is God when it hurts?' Busy thoughts, says an old translation of this psalm by William Kay, busy thoughts that multiply within me (v. 19). Sometimes the thoughts fill me with fear; sometimes they make me feel I might go mad! As I read some of the verses from this psalm, I try to offer these thoughts to God, for him to deal with.

### MONDAY

**Unless the LORD had given me help, I would soon have dwelt in the silence of death.**

*Psalm 94:17 (NIV)*

My thoughts are busy with my sorrow and tears, my remembering and my grief. My head aches with them and they drag me down. They silence the outside world until it feels like the silence of death. Unless the Lord helps me, I am helpless to do other than be busy with these thoughts.

*Please help me, Lord, and still my mind.*

## TUESDAY

**When I said, 'My foot is slipping,' your unfailing love, LORD, supported me.**

*Psalm 94:18 (NIV)*

Some days it feels as though my feet are slipping away underneath me and then I just want to stay in bed all day, wrapping the duvet about my ears, refusing to stand and face the reality of what has happened. And how disappointed I am that ___ has gone.

And yet – your love, O Lord, can and will support me. If I allow myself to feel your love.

*Please can I sense your arms of love holding me up today? Feel your support?*

## WEDNESDAY

**When the cares of my heart are many, your consolations cheer my soul.**

*Psalm 94:19 (ESV)*

The cares of my heart, the busy-ness of my thoughts, exhaust me again and again. They occupy me most of the time. They prevent my sleep, they focus away from food, they shut me off from others.

Memories.

Regrets and remembrances. The without-ness, the emptiness. Wanting one last hug, one last look, one last together-time. Don't go there. I must. I can't not.

But – *'Thy consolations have soothed my soul.'* (v. 19, LXX) I can't feel the joy, the cheer, not yet, not even in your strong consolation, dear Lord. But I know that I will. Soon.

*Thank you for consoling me as no other can. Please let me feel your consolation soothing my soul today.*

## THURSDAY

**The LORD is my fortress – stronghold – defence – high tower – defender . . .**

*Psalm 94:22 (NIV, ISV, KJV, AMP, NCV)*

The translations each have something for me to hold on to. A fortress, where I can find safety and security behind its thick walls. A stronghold, unassailable from attack. A high tower, way above the rushing waters of grief and busy thoughts. A defence and a defender. Somewhere safe when I have thoughts of fear and instability.

*I want to run into the Lord and be saved from the raging torrent of grief.*

## FRIDAY

**. . . my God is the mighty rock where I hide.**

*Psalm 94:22 (NLT)*

A rock gives shade from the intense heat of the scorching desert. Sometimes my grief makes me feel as parched and dry as the Sahara. A rock also can be a place to climb, to escape from the waters below.

*Lord, you are my shade in the desert, my safety in the floods. Hide me in you today.*

## SATURDAY

**When I was upset and beside myself, you calmed me down and cheered me up.**

*Psalm 94:19 (MSG)*

That's exactly how it feels, heavenly Father – I am 'upset and beside myself' so often at the moment. But you can calm me down and cheer me up.

*I'm turning to you, yet again, knowing that you are all I need. Knowing that you can still these busy thoughts, quieten my grief, strengthen my weakness, cheer me up because I trust in you. Thank you, Lord.*

# THE WATERS OF GRIEF
## causing fear of drowning

The waters of grief ebb and flow. A tear can become a waterfall; the gentle wave lapping at my toes turns without warning and crashes down over me. Grief can make me panic or be hyperactive; it makes me forget things. Or makes me fearful in great waves of fear.

*Isaiah writes for this.*

## MONDAY

**Fear not . . .**                                   *Isaiah 43:1 (KJV)*

My grief causes extraordinary emotions, ones I hadn't realised it would bring. Tiredness, yes; but there's caution and self-doubt and fear. Inability to do this – and this – and this. I hesitate now, fearful I can't do that – or that.

Isaiah writes that the Lord says: ***fear not***. Don't be afraid! Jesus said it several times,[3] as well. It's in the Bible many times – don't be afraid, don't worry, don't be anxious. Fear not. But I do; I do fear, I do feel afraid.

*Let me hear the reassurance of your loving voice, Lord, gently giving me confidence in you. Let me hear you speaking to me today.*

## TUESDAY

**I have called you by name. You are mine.**

*Isaiah 43:1 (ESV)*

These words give me a sense of intimacy, of a deep relationship with you, my heavenly Father. I belong to you. Even though I feel unable, dis-abled, by this deep mourning, you care deeply for me.

I am redeemed by Christ and called by grace; loved and cherished by you.

*Now, when I mourn the loss of earthly love and relationship, help me to know, to feel, loved and accepted by you.*

## WEDNESDAY

**When you go through deep waters, I will be with you.**

*Isaiah 43:2 (NLT)*

I'm surely going through deep waters! Sometimes I am wading; sometimes I am swimming; sometimes it feels as though I am about to go right under. Those huge waves and breakers of grief wash over me, often at unexpected moments.

It feels very lonely sometimes.

But these words today tell me that you're here with me, Lord – not taking me *out* of the waters, but going *through* them with me.

*Thank you, thank you for accompanying me, swimming with me, in these deep waters.*

## THURSDAY

**When you go through rivers of difficulty, you will not drown.**

*Isaiah 43:2 (NLT)*

Oh, but I *am* drowning, God!

Sometimes it's almost impossible to breathe, my chest is tight and grief threatens to take over, to the point of drowning. I gasp for air, flounder; my feet give way under the immense pressure of the heavy waters of these rivers. I am going under . . .

And then I feel your arms around me, rescuing me, keeping me afloat, dragging me to safety.

For now. Until the next time. For there is still wave upon wave upon wave ahead.

*You've promised I will not drown. Can I trust you to save me again and again? I choose to trust you, Lord; please keep my head above water!*

## FRIDAY

**For I am the LORD your God . . . your Savior. . . . you are precious to me, you are honored and I love you.**

*Isaiah 43:3-4 (GWT)*

Those words speak deep healing into my sad soul today. The Almighty God, the 'King of kings and Lord of lords' (Revelation 19:16[4]), says that I am precious to him, honoured and loved by him.

I need to think quietly about this, turn those words over in my mind and my heart, take them with me into today.

*Say those words to me again, Lord. That I am precious to you and you love me.*

## SATURDAY

**Do not be afraid, for I am with you.**

*Isaiah 43:5 (NLT)*

Those words of reassurance again, reiterating what I need to hear – that you're with me in and through all this, Lord. As the waters threaten me today, may I remember that you're with me, you love me, I am precious to you, and you won't let me drown.

*Come rescue me again! I'm clinging to you in the waters of grief today. Thank you for being stronger than any waters which may threaten me.*

# CLOSE TO ME

## together in Christ

Jesus promised that when believers die, they go to be with him. He also promised to be always with us. If our loved ones are with him and he is with us, they cannot be so very far away. We are together in Him.

### MONDAY

**Don't let your hearts be troubled. Trust in God, and trust also in me.**

*John 14:1 (NLT)*

My heart is troubled, very troubled. The disciples were worried and upset because Jesus was talking about leaving them, and they were already beginning to feel the loss of this friendship and leadership and relationship.

So he reassures them – and reminds them to trust. And then to trust some more. I know I need to trust, but knowing it and doing it are not the same.

*Jesus, I want to trust you today, to know that you will comfort me and be with me even in the loneliest of moments.*

## TUESDAY

**My Father's house has many rooms; if that were not so, would I have told you that I am going there to prepare a place for you?**

*John 14:2 (NIV)*

I love the thought of Jesus going ahead and preparing somewhere special for me. And for my loved ones. I don't need to be overwhelmed by the sorrow of this time. They are already in the special places he has prepared for them. What it is like, I don't need to know now, but it is comforting to think they're already enjoying what he's prepared just for them.

*Thank you, Jesus, that I can trust your words to be true. Thank you for preparing a special place for ___ and one for me too when I come home.*

## WEDNESDAY

**When everything is ready, I will come and get you, so that you will always be with me where I am.**

*John 14:3 (NLT)*

'Come' is present tense – so it's not referring to your Second Coming in glory but to the present time. You came for ___ because their place was ready. And they are always with you. But I'm still here, without them, and it's really hard. People keep telling me that they are 'in a better place,' and so they are; but I'm not and I miss them very, very much.

*Lord, help me to be glad for \_\_\_ and to be thankful that they're with you; help me to be patient until the time when you come for me.*

## THURSDAY

**And I will ask the Father, and he will give you another Helper, to be with you for ever . . . He is the Holy Spirit, who . . . lives with you now and later will be in you.**

*John 14: 16 (ESV), 17 (NLT)*

**I will not leave you comfortless; I will come to you.**

*John 14:18 (KJV)*

If 'come' is in the present tense, then, Lord Jesus, it also means that you come to us. To me. You promised to come and I believe you do. You come by the power of your Spirit and you promised not to leave me 'comfortless.'

That's another of the promises that I claim:

*Come to me, Lord Jesus, with the comfort only you can give.*

## FRIDAY

**I am leaving you with a gift – peace of mind and heart. And the peace I give is a gift the world cannot give. So don't be troubled or afraid.**

*John 14:27 (NLT)*

You remind me not to be troubled or upset. Yet I am, Lord, and I need your gift of 'peace of mind and heart' today.

Remind me of your words as I try to act normally; as I meet people, as I interact with the world.

*Grant me your gift of peace and may I BE a gift to others too, in whatever way I can.*

## SATURDAY

**And be sure of this: I am with you always, even to the end of the age.**

*Matthew 28:20 (NLT)*

So there it is: they are with you, Lord, and you are with me – they cannot be very far away. Thank you that we're together in you; thank you that you're with me.

*I need to feel your closeness to me today, Lord.*

# WHAT OF THOSE WHO DIE WITHOUT CHRIST?

Jesus made a promise that when we die, we go to be with Him. He also promised that He is always with us.

Our loved ones are with Him and He is with us – so they are not very far away.

We are held in Him together.

But what if ___ didn't acknowledge Christ? What then? I believe I can still hold them to God, trusting in his grace and mercy and love. Asking for comfort for myself too.

And we none of us know exactly what happens at death, nor what other's perceptions of God might be. But I DO know that God is love, and that nothing, nothing, 'can . . . separate us from [his] love,' not even death (Romans 8:38-39, NLT) and that God works outside of our own perception of time. He is far bigger than we know, beyond time and space.

And he doesn't just *show* grace and love and mercy – he IS grace and love and mercy. So we may well be surprised when we discover who else is also in heaven!

*Meanwhile, I can give thanks for every memory of love, light and joy in ___ 's life, for the times we shared, for the moments that were good.*

*And I can continue to trust ___ to God's love, as he is a God who can be trusted. He is Alpha and Omega,[5] the God of all our beginnings and endings.*

# THE TWENTY-THIRD PSALM

## unruly emotions

There are some theories that grief goes through a neatly ordered set of emotions; from denial and anger, through bargaining, then on to depression and finally acceptance.

And for some who grieve that may be true. But for many people, sorrow and grief cannot be ordered or put into neat boxes. They are not stairs to be climbed where each step leaves the others behind as we move on and up. Emotions, perhaps especially grief, bounce around, ebb and flow, refuse to be corralled. Grief is untidy, messy, raw. It is a sea, one moment regular, the next whipped into crashing breakers, life-threatening and all-consuming in its rage.

Two months into mourning and the world moves on. Even Job's comforters only sat in silence with him for a mere seven days. The world urges us to 'pick up the threads again' because 'she wouldn't want you to be like this' or 'you need to get on with your life again.'

Not so, I silently retort. This is my time for grief, for remembrance, for mourning what I have lost.

Psalm 23 is often quoted as a gentle pastoral aid for grief, a reminder of 'green pastures,' gentle brooks, pleasant ways. Even the 'valley of the shadow of death' was not to be feared.

Sometimes I seemed to be walking in a different valley.

# PSALM 23: The Amplified Bible[6]

## MONDAY

**1 The Lord is my Shepherd [to feed, guide, and shield me], I shall not lack.**

But I DO lack, dear Shepherd! I lack the beloved presence – voice, glance, touch. All I can think about it is my without-ness. Through my tears, I'm unable to see you ahead of me, feeding, guiding, shielding me. My head knows you're there, but my heart can't feel you.

*Help me today to know the truth that you ARE there, that you are MY Shepherd; and that you care for this sad little sheep of your flock. Be my Shepherd today.*

## TUESDAY

**2 He makes me lie down in [fresh, tender] green pastures; He leads me beside the still and restful waters.**

My tendency right now is far from lying refreshed! Either I am restlessly moving, trying to fill the emptiness; or I am lethargically worn out from this all-consuming grief.

Be my Shepherd and please, please make me take time to be refreshed by you. The only waters I can sense are tumultuous and raging; lead me, dear Shepherd, to the places of your choosing. How I long for the refreshment that only you can give!

*Help me to accept your refreshment today. To know it's OK not to be OK. But also, to know you MAKE me rest!*

## WEDNESDAY

**3-4a He refreshes and restores my life (my self); He leads me in the paths of righteousness [uprightness and right standing with Him – not for my earning it, but] for His name's sake. Yes, though I walk through the [deep, sunless] valley of the shadow of death . . .**

Sometimes it feels as though I'm in the parched desert in the heat of the noonday sun. I yearn for the shade and a sip of water; but I have to walk this scorching way. And other days I'm frozen in a sunless valley, cold in the shadows of death.

*You, Lord, know how it feels; and you alone can give me the refreshment I crave. Be my Shepherd, lead me out of the deep, dark places. Restore me with your refreshment today. Show me your treasure in the dark places of my grief.*

## THURSDAY

**4b . . . I will fear or dread no evil, for You are with me; Your rod [to protect] and Your staff [to guide], they comfort me.**

Sometimes it feels as though I'm in the deepest, darkest valley, at the bottom of the steepest pit. It's cold and lonely. Death stands between me and my beloved. And death is the wild attacker, it knocks me off course.

But you, my Shepherd, have the rod to fight off the predator; you wield the staff to bang against the sides of the enclosing darkness and test out the safest way.

Even though I feel no comfort, that does comfort me. Because you are down here with me. You know what I'm going through. You do know.

*Protect me today, my Shepherd, from any attacks of grief that undermine my relationship with you.*

## FRIDAY

**5 You prepare a table before me in the presence of my enemies. You anoint my head with oil; my [brimming] cup runs over.**

When the enemy is trying to attack me in the dark wild places, I know you, my Shepherd, want to give me good things. It's hard to believe right now; but you care enough to massage my matted fleece with soothing oils and to serve me by looking after my needs, even when I am feeling so low. Your loving care of and for me is amazing.

*Thank you, Lord, for your love and care and protection – even in the deepest valley.*

## SATURDAY

**6 Surely or only goodness, mercy, and unfailing love shall follow me all the days of my life, and through the length of my days the house of the Lord [and His presence] shall be my dwelling place.**

Through all my days, no matter what I go through or am going through, your love for me, dear Shepherd, never fails. I can look back to times when I knew that love in extraordinary ways; I can anticipate that one day, I'll experience your love afresh. And yet your love is always there, always with me, always available. I can be in your presence all the time – wherever you lead me, whatever I go through, whoever is with me.

*Today I choose this: Your beloved presence as my Shepherd, even in this dark valley. Thank you for being in it with me.*

# THE LORD CARES DEEPLY
## when his loved ones die

Two things stand out in the first few weeks of my terrible traumatic loss and grief. First, there was a sense of not letting go – keep hold; hold it in; hold it very tight. There were things to do, a house to clear (in just three weeks, a whole lifetime's things to ponder, divide, dispense, jettison), people to contact, insurance claims to file. And secondly, a sense of being cold; frozen, even. My heart was frozen and it chilled me through. Not for a few weeks did I realise how cold I was the whole time, until I had a special treat: a facial, while my body was enveloped in warm towels and blankets. As I drifted in and out of drowsiness, I had an overwhelming sense of my grandmother and my father meeting my mother, and of the Lord welcoming her Home – the full 'dream' or 'living picture' is too intensely personal to share. How the Lord was wiping the tears from her eyes as she looked back at what she was being wrenched from. Wiped from hers; but not from mine, not yet. And for the first time ever there was a wistfulness, a longing, so quickly flashing through me, to be Home as well, to be with those beloved people. And then it was gone, the vision faded, and I was left in this world.

## MONDAY

**He will swallow up death for ever. The Sovereign LORD will wipe away the tears from all faces . . . Surely this is our God . . .**

*Isaiah 25:8-9 (NIV)*

I have to believe this promise, Sovereign Lord. That one day, death will be no more; there'll be no more dying, no more pain, no more tears.

And this picture of you as a loving parent, stooping tenderly to wipe away the ravages of grief on my face, fills me with peace and comfort.

*Yes, you are my God, my loving, caring, tender heavenly Father, who wipes away my tears.*

## TUESDAY

**If the dead are not raised, then Christ has not been raised either . . . But Christ has indeed been raised from the dead . . .**

*1 Corinthians 15:16,20 (NIV)*

This is part of our Christian faith and belief – Christ was raised from the dead, and therefore believers are also raised in him from the dead.

I can live, sleep, work, believe, as a Christian, and I will one day die like a Christian. Songs and rejoicings can be on my lips even if not yet in my heart. I *have* to believe that my loved one is with Christ.

One day I'll know it beyond the shadow of a doubt. For now, I cling on to that hope because it is my belief – because God's Word tells me it is true.

*Thank you that Jesus was raised from the dead and that one day we will all be with him for ever.*

## WEDNESDAY

**Our bodies are buried in brokenness, but they will be raised in glory . . . raised in strength . . . raised as spiritual bodies.**

*1 Corinthians 15:42-44 (NLT)*

And this is what God's Word tells me has happened to my loved one – living for ever, eternally, in glory and power. I have to learn to be grateful for that. I can't pretend it's not hard. I can't pretend other than that I would rather they were still here, with me, on earth. And yet, and yet . . . death is another beginning, not an end, for them, and will one day be so for me. It is what we have to look forward to.

In the meantime, ___ has simply changed addresses.

*Thank you, God, for giving us the 'victory over sin and death through our Lord Jesus Christ!' (v. 57)*

## THURSDAY

**LORD, be gracious to us; we long for you. Be our strength every morning, our salvation in times of distress.**

*Isaiah 33:2 (NIV)*

The verses of the past few days have highlighted to me one of the paradoxes of the Christian life – that it's better to be with the Lord and so it must be better for my loved one to be with him; and yet it's so painful and sorrowful to be parted and to be the one who is left here.

*Lord, I long for you to be my strength in this time of distress. I long to feel again your grace and love and tenderness.*

## FRIDAY

**Precious in the sight of the LORD is the death of his saints.**

*Psalm 116:15 (ESV)*

*or*

**The LORD cares deeply when his loved ones die.** *(NLT)*

Thank you, Lord, that you care; thank you that when your beloved ones come to you, it is a special and precious thing for you. It's hard for those of us left behind; but amazing that it is such a momentous and incredible occasion in heaven.

*Help me to be more grateful for that, Lord God. I know that gratitude is a great antidote to self-pity – and in grief I am especially prone to it. And I know that if we don't say goodbye here, we can't meet together in him, there.*

## SATURDAY

*Psalm 69*
**I wept soul tears.** *v. 10 (William Kay)*

**I will praise God's name in song and glorify him with thanksgiving.**

*v. 30 (NIV)*

**You who seek God, let your hearts revive.** *v. 32 (ESV)*

Deep, deep tears – and yet as in so many of the psalms, an experience of deep distress leads to looking upwards in praise and glory and worship and thanksgiving.

In my heart of hearts, I know this is the only way to be able to carry on. It revives and refreshes my spirit, comforts and calms my heart.

*Thank you, thank you. Let me keep on looking to you. I WILL praise your name, God.*

# PRAYING FOR THOSE WHO HAVE DIED

I don't pray enough for my loved ones; my mother used to pray for each of her children and each of her grandchildren and each of her great-grandchildren at least twice a day. Morning and evening, sitting in bed, she would spend time with her Lord and talk to him about her family. We prayed for one another; the habit of praying for the family members is deeply ingrained. But when they have died? My evangelical upbringing did not allow praying for the dead. Giving thanks for them, yes, remembering them with gratitude, yes. But not specifically praying for them. Until I was in the deepest grief and began reading about bereavement and dying and going to be with the Lord – and praying for and with those already in the Lord's presence.

## MONDAY

**For we know that when this earthly tent we live in is taken down (that is, when we die and leave this earthly body), we will have a house in heaven, an eternal body made for us by God himself and not by human hands.**

*2 Corinthians 5:1 (NLT)*

Yes, God – I know and believe that my loved one is with you, in the house in heaven which Jesus went to get ready when he left this world. And I know that death isn't the end, it's a new beginning, the most important beginning, the beginning of eternal life with you.

And love, love which makes life here on earth glorious and loving, cannot, does not, die. Love is eternal.

\_\_\_ has left the shabby tent of the earthly body and is now in the most glorious house, home, palace, with you.

*And I give you thanks for that.*

## TUESDAY

**I am torn . . . I desire to depart and be with Christ, which is better by far . . .**

*Philippians 1:23 (NIV)*

Paul could write that to die and be with Christ would be far better than continuing to live here. The biblical descriptions of heaven are of such a wonderful, glorious, loving, place. My loved one is gazing upon the face of the Lord. It's far better – for them.

*I give you thanks for that.*

## WEDNESDAY

**For anyone who enters God's rest also rests from their works, just as God did from his.**

*Hebrews 4:10 (NIV)*

I know that some believe that the Christian departed are in a state of 'restful happiness' awaiting the triumphal Second Coming of Christ. And so it is a comfort to me to be able to hold \_\_\_ in my prayer before the Lord; I hold him/her in my love, praying for refreshment, as they rest in God's love. I can be glad that _____ is at rest.

*I give you thanks for that.*

## THURSDAY

**Then I heard a voice from heaven say, 'Write this: blessed are the dead who die in the Lord from now on.'**

**'Yes,' says the Spirit, 'they will rest from their labour, for their deeds will follow them.'**

*Revelation 14:13 (NIV)*

Death was a shock to me. Whether death is sudden or not, unexpected or not, it's always a shock. But there's comfort to me to know that my loved one is blessed by you, resting, no longer having to *DO* anything, just *BEing* in you and in your loving and loved Presence. S/He no longer has to do all that heavy stuff they were burdened with here. Now they're resting. Continue to bless them, Lord.

*I give you thanks for that.*

## FRIDAY

**Love is invincible facing danger and death. . . . Flood waters can't drown love, torrents of rain can't put it out.**

*Songs 8:7 (MSG)*

I'm warmed by these words, to know that love does not die; love is eternal. There's nothing death can do to it. My ___ loved me a moment ago, passionately and completely. And who is to say that their love is not still loving me, loving me forever; for love does not forget. 'Many waters cannot quench love' (Song of Solomon 8:7, NIV); and I still love! In that love, both given and received, I hold my beloved within the love of God.

*I give you thanks for that.*

## SATURDAY

**Love never ends.** *1 Corinthians 13: 8 (ESV)*

**Love never gives up, never loses faith, is always hopeful, and endures through every circumstance.**

*1 Corinthians 13:7 (NLT)*

Love, mine for my loved one and theirs for me, becomes a prayer. Love never gives up. Our love – I know, I trust – will never end, always endure. 'Love never ends.'

*I give you thanks for that.*

# THE COMMUNION OF SAINTS

## surrounded by a great cloud of witnesses

Most of my life, I have repeated the Creed in church, including the phrase 'I believe in the communion of saints' (BCP).[7] And I did. In theory. But now, each time I come to that phrase, I say it with added depth and meaning. Because now I truly know what it means. It brings a new comfort to my broken, grieving heart.

### MONDAY

**Since we are surrounded by so great a cloud of witnesses . . .**

*Hebrews 12:1 (ESV)*

Scripture doesn't seem to tell us exactly how much of what goes on in our everyday lives is actually 'seen' by those who are already forever with the Lord. But it does tell us that they are like a great cloud around us, or maybe like the great crowd of spectators at the ancient Roman games. They are cheering us on! What a great encouragement to me, to know that ___ is in that cloud, part of the heartening inspiration to enable me to carry on.

*Lord, help me to live today knowing that the great 'cloud of witnesses,' including ___, is spurring me on!*

## TUESDAY

**[God] the Father, from whom every family in heaven and on earth derives its name.**

*Ephesians 3:14-15 (NIV)*

The family of God has some members in heaven and some still on earth. But it is not two different entities. We're all part of the same family.

*What comfort, Lord, to know that we are still together in you, still part of your family, together in Christ.*

## WEDNESDAY

**Now, dear brothers and sisters, let us clarify some things about the coming of our Lord Jesus Christ and how we will be gathered to meet him.**

*2 Thessalonians 2:1 (NLT)*

One day, when Christ comes again in glory, we'll all be gathered together – those who've already died and those still alive on earth – and we will *TOGETHER* meet him.

I can't imagine how that will feel; the glory and the joy and the love and the amazement! The tears wiped away and the pain gone for ever!

But I can echo the prayer in Revelation 22:20:

*Come quickly, Lord Jesus!*

## THURSDAY

Jesus promised:

**'And he will send out his angels with the mighty blast of a trumpet, and they will gather his chosen ones from all over the world – from the farthest ends of the earth and heaven.'**

*Matthew 24:31 (NLT)*

Another description, like yesterday's verse, with the promise that we will be joined and gathered together in the Lord at the Second Coming.

And something in me tells me that the great 'cloud of witnesses', who are surrounding me and inspiring me, and who will be gathered up with me, will be cheering as my feet step over the threshold into eternity with them. Together for ever.

*Come quickly, Lord Jesus!*

## FRIDAY

**For God had something better in mind for us, so that they would not reach perfection without us.**

*Hebrews 11:40 (NLT)*

The true communion of saints – they need us as much as we need them. They are waiting for us to join them and only then will God bring us all to what he's planned for eternity. Only together with us will they be perfect. So ____ and I, together with all the saints, will be for ever with the Lord.

**Therefore, comfort one another with these words,** writes Paul.

*(1 Thessalonians 4:18, NASB)*

*Come quickly, Lord Jesus!*

## SATURDAY

**After that, we who are still alive and are left will be caught up together with them in the clouds to meet the Lord in the air. And so we will be with the Lord for ever.**

*1 Thessalonians 4:17 (NIV)*

I know that this separation is temporary. And the reunion will be for ever! Even better, we will be *with the Lord* together, for ever.

I can't really imagine what that will be like. Except that it sounds glorious and wonderful. We will be with the Lord for ever.

*Thank you, Lord, that one day we all will be together with you for ever.*

# WALKING THROUGH THE VALLEY OF THE SHADOW
## three months of grief

It's now about three months. Three months of grief, aloneness, of walking through the 'valley of the shadow of death' (Psalm 34:4, AMP). The world around me seems already to have forgotten my loss and moved on.

Or, maybe it's just that they don't know what to say to me: they have said all the usual jargons and clichés of supposedly comforting words, and there is nothing more to be said.

Psalm 23 comes back to my mind again – even though I am (still) walking through this 'valley of the shadow of death,' and even though I know I have to take every single step in order to get to the end of it and see the light again – even through all this, the Good Shepherd is with me, to comfort me.

### MONDAY

**I am bowed down (miserable, depressed, troubled, in other versions[8]) and brought very low; all day long I go about mourning.**

*Psalm 38:6 (NIV)*

I can't seem to help this, Lord. I do indeed feel very low and alone, my only companion my mourning. It's like a roller coaster – some

99

days are better than others. I can't feel the sympathy and love that others have tried to give me. And sometimes I am still frozen in my grief.

*Lord, have mercy upon me.*

## TUESDAY

**I am exhausted and completely crushed. My groans come from an anguished heart.**

*Psalm 38:8 (NLT)*

The exhausted-ness of the psalmist can be translated as cold, without warmth. And that's exactly how it feels, Lord. I am cold, chilled through, by this burden of grief.

*Lord, have mercy upon me.*

## WEDNESDAY

**Casting all your care upon him; for he careth for you.**

*1 Peter 5:7 (KJV)*

I feel as if I have no strength! I feel in danger of being crushed by my burden of grief. It's heavy. All I can do is 'cast' it on to you, Lord; throw it, transfer it, to you to carry.

That's not easy to do and maybe I want to carry it myself! So I picture you, Lord, carrying me while I carry my grief.

*Lord, have mercy upon me and carry my grief with and for me.*

## THURSDAY

**O Lord, all my longing is before you; my sighing is not hidden from you.**

*Psalm 38:9 (ESV)*

That simply, says it all. I can't find the words to pray, Lord, but you know that. And what do words matter, when my longing, 'my desire' (KJV) is already before you, known to you.

*Lord, have mercy upon me.*

## FRIDAY

**My heart pounds, my strength fails me; even the light has gone from my eyes.**

*Psalm 38:10 (NIV)*

Someone said to me the other day that my eyes showed my pain and my grief, and no longer sparkle. I know; they are dull and lifeless and bruised with tears. And my strength fails, especially when I see others who also loved ___ and are grieving too. I see the pain in their eyes, I see their tears and it's too much for me to see or to carry.

*Lord, have mercy upon me. And on them.*

## SATURDAY

**LORD, I wait for you; you will answer, Lord my God. . . .**
**LORD, do not forsake me; do not be far from me, my God.**
**Come quickly to help me, my Lord and my Saviour.**

*Psalm 38:15,21-22 (NIV)*

In all the weakness and the sadness, in all the weariness and the sorrow, I will choose to wait for my Saviour.

And I know and trust that he will indeed come to my help and carry me.

*Lord, have mercy upon me.*

# PEACE

## which passes all understanding

Jesus said,
**'I have told you these things, so that in me you may have peace. In this world you will have trouble. But take heart! I have overcome the world.'**

*John 16:33 (NIV)*

This week, just these few words will be carried with me, for me to hold and meditate on, to have Christ's peace at the heart of all I feel. Just like chewing the cud, I want to extract every ounce of goodness, of strength and peace, from these few words.

### MONDAY

**. . . that in me you may have peace.**

I crave your peace, Jesus. As I go into this new week, with all that it holds, I long to know the peace which 'passes all understanding.'[9] Peace in and through the valley of shadows.

*Give me the peace you promised, Lord Jesus. Please!*

## TUESDAY

**. . . that in me you may have peace.**

I know in my head that peace does not come from circumstances (which change) or people (who can alter or depart) but only in Christ: the One who never changes.

*Help me to know that in my heart too. Give me the peace you promised, Lord Jesus. Please!*

## WEDNESDAY

**Here on earth you will have many trials and sorrows.** **(NLT)**

Yes. And this one in particular. I feel rather in limbo – held in a place of grief, where it's difficult to make decisions or do very much at all.

People tell me to be kind to myself; it's still early days. I guess they are right and I must accept that I can't do very much at the moment. And that's OK. For now.

*Give me the peace you promised, Lord Jesus. Please!*

## THURSDAY

**Here on earth you will have many trials and sorrows.** **(NLT)**

Thank you, Lord, that you knew there would be 'trials and sorrows' and that therefore I would need your peace to give me the security I need so desperately right now.

*May I know your peace again today, Lord, just as you promised.*

## FRIDAY

**But take heart! I have overcome the world.**

I don't like being so low, so overcome by my grief. I long to 'take heart' and feel more cheerful. Yet in some ways that seems almost to be letting my loved one down. I have a heart full of unshed tears, can't-shed tears.

*Lord, dry my tears with your peace. Give me the peace you promised, Lord Jesus. Please!*

## SATURDAY

**But take courage; I have overcome the world.** **(NASB)**

**But Jesus was quick to comfort them. 'Courage, it's me. Don't be afraid.'**

**Matthew 14:27 (MSG)**

When severe storm waves were battering at the disciples in their boat, and they must have felt abandoned by their Master, Jesus calmly walked out to them and told them not to be afraid – to have courage. I'm holding on to this today, Jesus, as I have all week, carrying it with me wherever I go. Give me your courage, your peace, and faith in you because you overcame the world when you defeated death and rose again. You overcome my storms.

*I'm grabbing hold of your peace and courage today, Lord Jesus! Thank you for your promise to give me your peace.*

# GOD'S ARMS AROUND ME
## wanting to know God's help

The prophetic words of Isaiah 33:2 were written to express how the Jewish nation felt when they were threatened by an invasion from Assyria. These are deep, heartfelt words, longing for God to rescue and support them, and put an end to their anxiety and distress. These words speak to me in my grief, and in my longing to know God helping and supporting me as I go through these deep waters.

> **LORD, be gracious to us; we long for you. Be our strength every morning, our salvation in times of distress.**
>
> *Isaiah 33:2 (NIV)*

### MONDAY

**LORD, be gracious to us ('have pity on us,' GWT); we long for you.**

I know you are faithful and your love is eternal, dear God. And you're gracious and take time to comfort me. My heart feels as though it is broken and I need you to tenderly heal it.

*I long for you.*

## TUESDAY

**We wait with hope for you.** *(GWT)*

Sometimes hope seems far away, and it's hard to wait. Lord Jesus, restore my faith in you and in your promise of life after death.

*I long for you.*

## WEDNESDAY

**Be our strength every morning . . .**

The mornings can be hard – waking up to the memory of my grief and who I'm missing. I need your strength this morning and I need it all day, too, Lord! I need it specially today with ......
 I invite you into my day, all through the day, knowing that you have all that I need. When I am weak through grief, your strength is sufficient. Thank you that you're constantly my strength and support.

*I long for you.*

## THURSDAY

**Be our arm every morning . . .** *(ESV)*

I love the picture of you extending your arm to me, Lord, so I can lean on you for support. Your arm is around me to protect me, and I depend on you today. I'm going to lean on you, hang on to your arm, feel myself propped up by your loving arm around me.

*I long to feel your arm around me today, Lord!*

## FRIDAY

**God, treat us kindly. You're our only hope. First thing in the morning, be there for us! When things go bad, help us out!**

**(MSG)**

You are indeed my only hope, Lord. I long for your kindness today, as I walk this lonely valley of grief. Pour your love and kindness over me.

*I long for more of your kindness. Let me feel you today!*

## SATURDAY

**Yes, be our savior in times of trouble.** **(GWT)**

I know that you're strong and that you save, God; I know that you're my Saviour. Today I want to reaffirm my belief in you and your strong arm. You are in this time of trouble with me.

*Thank you for your presence beside me.*

# WHERE IS GOD WHEN IT HURTS?

## the God who sees

Sometimes bereavement, loss, grief, stems from the death of a loved one; sometimes it is a result of other losses – work, home, culture, for example. Someone who knew that kind of grief was a woman who lost her home, her work, her security; thrown out by an unkind, unrelenting boss, forced to leave and feeling like a failure, feeling inadequate and rejected, wondering if she could have acted differently – and wondering whether God had any idea of what had happened and where she was. Did God care? Did God see?

### MONDAY

**You are the God who sees me . . .**          *Genesis 16:13 (NIV)*

Hagar, used and misused by those who employed and owned her, at the end of her tether because she had run away to escape the misery at home, is pregnant, destitute and alone. But God saw; God saw her situation and God sent an angel to help her. Then Hagar called God *El Roi* – the God who sees me.

*El Roi, help me to know that you see – you see me in my grief and desolation.*

## TUESDAY

**Have I also (or have I not also) looked after him that seeth me?**

*(CC)* [10]

The literal translation implies that Hagar was looking for the Lord —
she had *looked after* him in the sense of *looking for*. In her misery, in
her grief, she wondered whether God was near, whether God knew.
Thinking of him, looking for him, revealed him to her. She discovered
that he sees her.

*El Roi, I look for you — please see me in my despair.*

## WEDNESDAY

**The angel of the LORD found Hagar . . .**

*Genesis 16:7 (NIV)*

Where is God when it hurts? When it seems he doesn't know,
doesn't care? Are his eyes shut, is he asleep? Because that's how it
feels.

Actually, God was looking for Hagar and sent an angel to her. He
knew; he cared; he saw.

*El Roi, I need an angel from you today, maybe a friend who
understands and cares, or an email, or a note, or a phone call. Or,
maybe just a sense of your nearness to me and my dearness to you.*

## THURSDAY

**You are to name him Ishmael . . .**                    *Genesis 16:11 (NLT)*

Ishmael, the child Hagar was carrying deep within her. Ishmael, whose names means *God hears*. Hagar had experienced God knowing her, God seeing her, God HEARING her cry for help.

*El Roi, hear my crying, my sorrow, my need for you as I call out to you. Thank you that you promise to hear when I cry to you.*

## FRIDAY

**The LORD has heard your cry of distress.**
                                    *Genesis 16:11 (NLT)*

Forever after, both Hagar and Ishmael would be reminded that God hears, because of the name of the boy, and then the man he became. *God hears.* 'The LORD has heard.'

*El Roi, you see me and you hear me. Thank you. May I be constantly reminded of that today.*

## SATURDAY

**Truly here I have seen him who looks after me.**
                                    *Genesis 16:13 (ESV)*

The result of God's comforting words was that Hagar knew without a shadow of doubt that the Lord was looking at her – looking out for her – looking after her.

*El Roi, may I know the truth of your looking today – and tomorrow, and always.*

# RAGING SEAS

## overwhelmed by grief

Grief is strange and changes us. Step by step we move through its different stages – whether we want to or not. Sometimes it feels as though I am becoming resigned to this state of sorrow; sometimes it rises up like a mighty ocean and crashes wave after wave upon me, and I am all but subsumed in the tidal waters of grief.

### MONDAY

**You rule over the surging sea; when its waves mount up, you still them.**

*Psalm 89:9 (NIV)*

The waters of grief pour over me, Lord. They are crashing about me, threatening me, almost subsuming me. But you are in control!

*Still the tempest, Lord; quieten me, in your love. Hold me like a mother holds her crying child, close and comforting.*

### TUESDAY

**The waves of death overwhelmed me; floods of destruction swept over me. . . . But in my distress I cried out to the LORD; yes, I cried to my God for help. He heard me from his sanctuary; my cry reached his ears.**

*2 Samuel 22:5,7 (NLT)*

That's exactly how it feels! Overwhelmingly destructive. I think David knew that feeling too, in this song describing how it felt to be overcome by raging grief.

What did he do?
*'In my distress I called to the LORD; I called out to my God. From his temple he heard my voice; my cry came to his ears.'*

*(NIV)*

*Lord, I'm calling out to you because the floods are sweeping over me. Hear me! Rescue me! Comfort me!*

## WEDNESDAY

**I would hurry to my place of shelter, far from the tempest and storm.**

*Psalm 55:8 (NIV)*

Some days I want to be far away from this season of my life, free from all of the tears and torrents of grief. I want to be sheltered from it all. I need a sanctuary.

Where can I go? Where is my place of shelter and quiet? Where is my 'walk in the country', my 'cabin in the woods'? (v. 8, MSG)

The Lord is a place of safety. He shelters me under his wing, like a mother hen. (Matthew 23:37)

*Thank you for being 'my place of shelter.' Thank you for sheltering me under your wing. Please let me feel you sheltering me today!*

## THURSDAY

**You are . . . a tower of refuge to the needy in distress. You are a refuge (or 'shelter,' NIV) from the storm . . .**

*Isaiah 25:4 (NLT)*

I know I need to allow the Lord to shelter me in this stormy sea of sorrow. Yet sometimes, perversely, there are days when I seem to *want* to be right in it, to feel the sorrow in all its power and depths, and not to be out of it, for that might feel like not being sorrowful enough.

Emotions are strange sometimes.

*Thank you for being my place of shelter. Thank you for sheltering me under your wing. Please let me feel you sheltering me today!*

## FRIDAY

**'Don't you care if we drown?' He got up, rebuked the wind and said to the waves, 'Quiet! Be still!'**

*Mark 4:39 (NIV)*

Sometimes it feels as though Jesus doesn't care if I drown! He's sleeping through it all. Trying to imagine the strong winds and the high waves and the tossing little fishing boat makes me think the disciples would have yelled at you, Lord! How else would they have got through to you?

I yell at you too, through the fury and the storm and the fear of grief. *Don't you care, Lord?*

He stands and because he *does* care, he quietens it all down for me. Just because I asked.

Or yelled.

*Do you care, Lord?*

*I know you do. Please still my raging emotions and fill me with your stillness and peace.*

## SATURDAY

**He got up and rebuked the wind and the raging waters; the storm subsided, and all was calm.**

*Luke 8:24 (NIV)*

Even the wind and waves obey you.[11] As I pass through this storm of my life, I know you're in control and you won't let me be drowned by it all. You rescue me and keep my head above the deep waters.

*Do you care, Lord? I know you do. Please still my raging emotions and fill me with your stillness and peace. Thank you for granting me your calm.*

# MELTED IN HIS SUNLOVE

## frozen with grief

Frost can outline and define the deadest of leaves and twigs – but it is not here to stay. Even in the middle of winter, a touch of sun will make the frost sparkle and will then melt it.

### MONDAY

**I pray to you, O LORD, my rock. Do not turn a deaf ear to me. For if you are silent, I might as well give up and die.**

*Psalm 28:1 (NLT)*

I feel dead sometimes – encrusted with ice and frost, dead to all emotion other than grief. Some days I am overwhelmingly frostbitten, lifeless.

*Don't let me die, Lord; let your sunlove bring me life.*

### TUESDAY

**Let your face shine on your servant; save me in your unfailing love.**

*Psalm 31:16 (NIV)*

I turn my face towards your sunlove, and know that your love is always there, always warm, always strengthening.

*Even at my most frozen, your love is pouring over me, O Lord.*

## WEDNESDAY

**Your unfailing love, O LORD, is as vast as the heavens; your faithfulness reaches beyond the clouds.**

*Psalm 36:5 (NLT)*

My heart can feel frozen still, Lord – but I look up at your immense heavens which show how vast is your love for me, and for my beloved.

*And I am grateful for all that you are to me.*

## THURSDAY

**Praise your God! . . . He spreads snow like a white fleece, he scatters frost like ashes, He broadcasts hail like birdseed – who can survive his winter? Then he gives the command and it all melts; he breathes on winter – suddenly it's spring!**

*Psalm 147:12-18 (MSG)*

I want to believe that promise, Lord – that one day soon it will feel like spring again, that even without my beloved, the warmth of your sunlove will bring new life once again.

*Thank you for promising to turn winter into spring. Thank you for the promise and gift of new life.*

## FRIDAY

**You let [everyone] drink from Your refreshing stream.**

*Psalm 36:8 (HCSB)*

*Even when the stream itself seems cold, the warmth of your love, dear Lord, rises to abundantly satisfy. May I be satisfied in you today.*

## SATURDAY

**Whatever I have, wherever I am, I can make it through anything in the One who makes me who I am.**

*Philippians 4:13 (MSG)*

I am in my grief – but it's you, Lord Christ, who defines me, defines who I am, not my grief. I am IN my grief but not OF it. I am of you and you are my strength.

*In you I can make it through today, tomorrow, to eternity and this is my prayer today.*

# LEARNING TO LEAN
## when I need to rest

Grief, all-consuming, is draining. I hadn't realised how tiring it is to mourn, how little I seem to be able to accomplish, how exhausting it is to do things I used to rush around and do comparatively easily. Sometimes I need to allow myself a quieter day, whether physically, spiritually or emotionally – to let go and allow God to be my all-in-all, my tower of strength.

### MONDAY

**He who trusts in, relies on, and confidently leans on the Lord shall be compassed about with mercy and with loving-kindness.**
*Psalm 32:10 (AMP Classic Edition)*

I love the idea of leaning – leaning into you, letting you take the weight, the strain, today, knowing that I'll be surrounded with your love. Leaning into you, under your arm, feeling your love throwing a cloak of protection around me.

Knowing your unfailing love surrounds the one who leans on you.

*Lord, I'm going to lean on you today. You'll have to prop me up!*

## TUESDAY

**When I am afraid, I put my trust in you.**

*Psalm 56:3 (NIV)*

*Many of the newer translations of this psalm use 'trust' where the word might originally have read 'lean.' Lean towards, lean into, lean against.*

When I'm afraid – afraid of the depth of my grief, afraid I'll never be the same again, afraid I'll never be confident and capable again, I lean on you, lean into you, lean against you.

*Lord, I'm going to lean on you today. You'll have to prop me up!*

## WEDNESDAY

**You will keep in perfect and constant peace the one whose mind is steadfast [that is, committed and focused on You – in both inclination and character] . . . Trust [confidently] in the LORD . . .**

*Isaiah 26:3-4 (AMP)*

I can trust confidently, lean confidently, on you because you won't give way, let me down, trip over or fall.
    When I lean into you, I have perfect and constant peace.
    Even in and through this storm.

*I'm learning to lean on you today, Lord. I'll fall over unless you hold me up. And I'm glad you won't fall over!*

## THURSDAY

**The LORD is my strength and my shield; my heart trusts in him, and he helps me . . . with my song I praise him.**

*Psalm 28:7 (NIV)*

My heart leans and I am helped; when I lean into you, Lord God, I'm able riskily to look up – and praise you.

*I'm leaning on you today, Lord! You are amazing to prop me up. Thank you for being strong enough to have me leaning against you!*

## FRIDAY

**Surely, it is God who saves me; I will trust in him and not be afraid. For the Lord is my stronghold and my sure defense, and he will be my Savior.**

*Isaiah 12:1-2 (Canticle 9: The First Song of Isaiah)[12]*

*This canticle has been set to a beautiful tune – I'm going to hum it throughout today as a reminder of leaning and trusting.*

You are a strong God, like a fortress built on a rock, fully able to hold me up when I lean on you. When I need to lean and let you take the strain, so that I can have a rest, you're always there for me.

*I'm leaning on you today, Lord! You are amazing to prop me up. Thank you for being strong enough to have me leaning against you!*

## SATURDAY

**Whoever leans on, trusts in, and is confident in the Lord – happy, blessed, and fortunate is he.**

*Proverbs 16:20 (AMP Classic Edition)*

I'm grateful you're a Saviour who is such a strength to me, on whom I can lean, and who gives me peace. Even if I don't always feel it now, I know you're there for me and I can lean into you whenever I need to. *Thank you, Lord!*

# THE HAND OF GOD
## Does God allow (or even cause) pain?

### MONDAY

**'I will not cause pain without allowing something new to be born,' says the Lord.**

*Isaiah 66:9 (NCV)*

Did – does – God *allow* this pain? Does he *cause* it? Sometimes it's very confusing; I don't know where the pain comes from, why God doesn't stop it. I *ache*, Lord, with this pain, deep, deep in me. I carry it around with me and there is no escaping. Might there be something new and good from it one day?

*Here's my pain and here are my tears. It's all I have to give you today, Lord.*

### TUESDAY

**But I am trusting you, O LORD, saying, 'You are my God!' My future is in your hands.**

*Psalm 31:14-15 (NLT)*

Corrie ten Boom is said to have told people that we should 'Never be afraid to trust an unknown future to a known God.'[13]

My future appears quite bleak at the moment, dear God, without \_\_\_ And yet I know I can say those words in verse 15, that 'my future is in your hands.'

That's very comforting, knowing that whatever the future holds, whatever it looks like, it's in your hands.

*Help me to trust in you, Lord – it's not easy today. I need to trust the future to you, knowing that whatever happens, you ARE in control.*

## WEDNESDAY

The Lord says:
**'See, I have written your name on the palms of my hands.'**
*Isaiah 49:16 (NLT)*

You love me so much that you haven't only written my name on your hand, but tattooed it there permanently. It's such a sign of your love and care for me!

*Lord, I know now that you won't forget me. You can't – my name is tattooed on your hand!*

## THURSDAY

**For I am the LORD your God who takes hold of your right hand and says to you, Do not fear; I will help you.**
*Isaiah 41:13 (NIV)*

What a picture of a loving father, holding a small child by the hand. I *AM* sometimes afraid – afraid of what this pain and grief might do to me. I need to know you as my loving heavenly Father holding my hand.

*Take my hand today, Lord and help me. I want to feel safe with you.*

## FRIDAY

**The Spirit of the Lord is upon me, because he hath anointed me to preach the gospel . . . he hath sent me to heal the brokenhearted . . .**

*Luke 4:18 (KJV)*

I am the broken-hearted. My heart is broken.

God, I know you can mend a broken heart – but I have to give you all the pieces, every single one. And that's not as easy as it sounds! I remember the beautiful bowl of hope, the pieces mended in the Kintsugi method where the resin is mixed with gold so that the broken bowl is mended to be beautiful in a different way, the cracks still there but filled with gold.

*Here's my little, broken heart, Lord. Every single piece of it. I'm trusting you to mend it in such a way that it will be an image of hope and beauty to others, mended with your gold.*

## SATURDAY

**The LORD's right hand has done mighty things!**

*Psalm 118:15 (NIV)*

I put myself in your strong hands, knowing that there is no safer place. Your hand has my name written on it. Your hands can mend a broken heart. Your hands are strong yet tender. Your hands will heal.

*Into Thy Hands.*
*Lord have mercy.*
*Thee I adore.*

Attributed to Thomas Traherne (1636-1674)[14]

# EL SHADDAI

## wanting to know that God is all-sufficient

There are several powerful descriptions of God's names in Scripture. El Shaddai, שׁדי אני אל is one of the best known – and perhaps one of the best loved – partly due to a song with this name of God repeated in its first lines.[15] Many people have known the power of El Shaddai, when they have run to God for comfort and strength.

### MONDAY

**The LORD appeared to him (Abraham) and said, 'I am El-Shaddai – "God Almighty."'**

*Genesis 17:1 (NLT)*

El Shaddai – It's sometimes thought to mean 'The All-Sufficient One.' The One who is powerful, who has infinite strength. Who has everything I need.

*Lord, I need to know you as my El Shaddai today: my powerful One.*

### TUESDAY

**I am the Almighty God . . .**    *Genesis 17:1 (KJV)*

*El* – this very old word for God means strength, might, power.
But *Shaddai* has a very different sense – this is the person who is the provider, the one who pours out all that is needed. Just as

a mother feeds her infant, and provides everything – strength and nourishment, love and contentment. The Lord God as a breastfeeding mother.

El Shaddai – the powerful provider of strength and comfort and nourishment.

*You are my El Shaddai. Please give me your strength and comfort and nourishment; I need them today.*

## WEDNESDAY

**I am God All-Sufficient.**                    *(Genesis 17:1)*[16]

Everything I need is found in you, my El Shaddai; you supply and satisfy. You are all sufficient and enough to satisfy my deepest longings, and to heal my hurts.

*Lord, I need to know you as my El Shaddai today: my sufficiency.*

## THURSDAY

**The sound of the wings of the cherubim could be heard as far away as the outer court, like the voice of God Almighty when he speaks.**

*Ezekiel 10:5 (NIV)*

Your voice, the voice of El Shaddai, is penetrating and far-reaching. You can even penetrate the thick fog of my grief and reach deeply into me – to bring your comfort, your love, your sufficiency.

*El Shaddai, I need to hear your voice. You'll need to be a foghorn to penetrate my tears today!*

## FRIDAY

**The LORD appeared to him and said, 'I am God Almighty; walk before me faithfully and be blameless.'**

*Genesis 17:1 (NIV)*

**Live in my presence with integrity.** *(GWT)*

God, my God, you are my provider, my comforter, my sustainer. You're all-powerful, all-sufficient. Your relationship with me is unconditional. I live in your presence, and I want to be blameless before you – living with integrity. Even in my grief.

*El Shaddai, I need you today: giving me strength to live with integrity in your presence. And remember to shout through my grief!*

## SATURDAY

**My grace is sufficient for you, for my power is made perfect in weakness.'**

*2 Corinthians 12:9 (NIV)*

*El Shaddai, thank you for your promise to be all-sufficient. Your grace is all that I need. You are indeed my El Shaddai. That's all I need to know today.*

# A NEW DAY DAWNING
## a daily remembering

Each new day dawns with the awakening moment of remembering. Each new remembering still hits hard, contracts my gut, releases tears. What will this new day bring in terms of memory, of pain, of loss? The anxious moment jumpstarts my day – unless I turn to the Lord.

### MONDAY

**Don't worry about anything; instead, pray about everything. Tell God what you need, and thank him for all he has done.**

***Philippians 4:6 (NLT)***

That could read, could sound, so glib:

Don't worry, just pray.

But it's true. Lord, this loss causes me anxiety about today, about every day. I bring that anxiety to you, thanking you for the good memories of happier days, of love and laughter in those long-lost moments.

*Here is my worry, my anxiety, my loss, Lord. My grief, really. Take it for me. Hold it for me. Hold me in the hollow of your hand.*[17]

## TUESDAY

**Then you will experience God's peace, which exceeds anything we can understand. His peace will guard your hearts and minds as you live in Christ Jesus.**

*Philippians 4:7 (NLT)*

Again, Lord, I hold out this worry, this anxiety, this loss, to you. Thank you for taking hold of it for me.

I long for your peace, the peace I need, yet can barely comprehend at the moment.

*Let it come, Lord! Let that peace you give pour over me now and through today.*

## WEDNESDAY

**Thy God hath sent forth strength for thee . . .**

*Psalm 68:28 (BCP)[18]*

Another new day, another time of not knowing what lies ahead. Another fear that I haven't the strength to meet the unknown, the unexpected, the reminder.

And yet now I know it will be all right, that all will be well – because my God (yes, mine, even mine) has already sent out the strength I need, ready for when I need it.

*Thank you for sending out the strength I need already! I'm taking hold of it as best I can!*

## THURSDAY

**My God with his lovingkindness will meet me . . .**

*Psalm 59:10 (ASV)*

That difficulty coming to meet me, that unexpected reminder, that clearing out of ___ 's things which I have to do – all that and more, I don't have to confront alone.

Before it can meet me, my God will meet me with all the love and kindness I need, poured out upon me.

*Meet me today, Lord. Meet me before I meet that anxious moment.*

## FRIDAY

**I cling to you; your strong right hand holds me securely.**

*Psalm 63:8 (NLT)*

*Cling* is the Hebrew word for glued or stuck to. It is also the word for following or chasing, in order to grab hold. So that's what I need to do today – stick myself to the Lord, and grab hold of him! Or maybe grab hold of him and then stick to him.

And make sure I don't let go of him.

*But could you please hold me securely – not let go of me? Because I may not have the strength to grab hold and cling on to you! Thank you that your right hand holds tightly on to me, not letting me fall or sink.*

## SATURDAY

**An angel from heaven appeared to him [Jesus] and strengthened him.**

*Luke 22:43 (NIV)*

It's a comfort to know that when there was a need for special strength, you, the Father, sent an angel to your Son, Jesus, even though Jesus had already said he had 'overcome the world' (John 16:33).

*Lord, I need your special strength to keep going through all of this. Thank you that I can tell you what I need; thank you for all you have already done.*

# ALL – ALWAYS

## is God really able?

**And God is able to make all grace abound to you, so that in all things at all times, having all that you need, you will abound in every good work.[19]**

*2 Corinthians 9:8 (NIV 1984)*

### MONDAY

**And God is able**

Do I believe that? Do I believe you, God, are able, *even in this grief of mine*, to do the best for me, to give me your grace, to comfort and strengthen me? And am I praying, living, walking, in that belief? Only by your grace.

*Give me grace, Lord, to trust in you today and to know that you are able to do far more than all I can 'ask or imagine.' (Ephesians 3:20, NIV)*

### TUESDAY

**to make all grace abound**

*All* means *all*, not some.

All the wonders and strength of your grace can 'abound' for me today.

That speaks to me of overflowing, abundant, even-more-than-I need-right-now and on-throughout-today grace!

Your grace is more than sufficient, it constantly pours out on me – like a Niagara Falls, like a flowing artesian well, like a never-ending fountain.

*Please make all grace abound to me today, Lord. All, not just some.*

## WEDNESDAY

### so that in all things

*All* means *all*, not some.

In all things, *even this*, even this grief and loss and bereavement, you reach out to me. Even to me. The cross of Christ is big enough *even for this*.

*May I know your grace today in all things, in everything I do, in everyone I meet.*

## THURSDAY

### at all times [always]

*All* means *all,* not some.

At all times today, wherever I am, whatever I am doing, whatever time it is, you're with me in this. *At all times.*

Older translations[20] say *Always. And always means always.* Not just sometimes. Grace abounds always.

*All through today, Lord, wherever I am, whatever I am doing, whatever time it is, may I know your presence with me and your grace abounding over me.*

## FRIDAY

### having all that you need

*All* means *all*, not some.

What do I need from God today? What special grace do I need from him? Who might I meet today who needs to see God in me? To whom might I extend grace from God today?

*Lord, please give me ALL that I need from you for today, wherever I am and whatever I am doing.*

## SATURDAY

### you will abound in every good work

You have promised to give me all I need, Lord God, so that I can overflow with your goodness in every good thing I do. Today I need more of your grace, your love, your comfort.

*Thank you, Lord, for your grace, which is all that I could ever possibly need and more. Thank you that it's available always, not just sometimes. Help me to use it for good in everything I do today.*

# GOING FORWARD

## giving thanks in the brokenness

'Though the mountains be shaken
and the hills be removed,
yet my unfailing love for you will not be shaken
nor my covenant of peace be removed,'
says the LORD, who has compassion on you.

*Isaiah 54:10 (NIV)*

### MONDAY

My soul is weary with sorrow; strengthen me according to your word.

*Psalm 119:28 (NIV)*

Open your mouth and taste, open your eyes and see – how good GOD is. Blessed are you who run to him.

*Psalm 34:8 (MSG)*

This journey of grief is a strange one and very tiring. I am indeed weary with sorrow. Maybe even weary OF sorrow. It's such a roller coaster and I never know whether the day will be up or down; and sometimes it's both. And that's tiring.

But this I know – YOU heal the broken-hearted! My broken, bruised and battered heart is in your hands and you are healing me. Life won't ever be the same without ___, yet I am learning to allow you to heal and restore and enable me to go forward in your strength. Your word to me gives new life and helps me in this new normal.

*I'm running to you again today, Lord! Thank you, that your word to me is strengthening and sustaining, and holds me up. Thank you for your promise to be with me.*

## TUESDAY

**My love won't walk away from you, my covenant commitment of peace won't fall apart.**

*Isaiah 54:10 (MSG)*

My grief doesn't follow rules. One minute I'm feeling fine, the next the grief comes crashing back and overwhelms me. It resurfaces just when I'm not expecting it, which can be disconcerting.

But you, Lord God, have promised me your peace! Sometimes I'm more aware of it than others.

*Don't walk away from me today, Lord. You promised not to and I'm holding on to your promise!*

## WEDNESDAY

**Even if the mountains walk away and the hills fall to pieces, my love won't walk away from you . . .**

*Isaiah 54:10 (MSG)*

Sometimes I'm so angry that you let this death happen, Lord God. Some days the anger is intense and all I can do is ask: WHY? Why death for ___ and why grief and sorrow for me? Why should they have to die? Why should I have to go through this terrible grief? Some days it feels like the end of the world, mountains and hills collapsing all around me.

Yet, you know! Even if it feels like the end of the world to me, you know and you care. You promise never to walk away from me, never to take your love away from me.

*When I'm angry at you, Lord, you still love me and care for me. Thank you for your promise never to walk away from me.*

## THURSDAY

**The GOD who has compassion on you . . .**

*Isaiah 54:10 (MSG)*

*Compassion: dictionaries define the word as a strong feeling of sympathy and love towards someone who is suffering, and a desire to share and reduce their suffering.*

If that's the meaning for earthly compassion, then I can know that your compassion is all that and much, much more! You feel deep compassion for me in my grief and want to share it with me and reduce it for me.

*Thank you, Lord, for your compassion and your desire to share and carry and reduce my suffering. Here it is; I'm welcoming your compassion today!*

## FRIDAY

**...the God of all comfort, who comforts and encourages us in every trouble so that we will be able to comfort and encourage those who are in any kind of trouble, with the comfort with which we ourselves are comforted by God.**

*2 Corinthians 1:3-4 (AMP)*

As I've praised you, Lord God, and reached out to you in the depths of my sorrow, you have comforted me, and encouraged me, and somehow my relationship with you has deepened.

It wasn't something I anticipated. Some days I've felt (and still feel) very far away from you, or it feels like you don't care. And yet — you *have* reached out to me, taken me deeper, and there are days and times when I've been able to praise you.

Who can I comfort and encourage today? This week? Who else needs to know the comfort and encouragement that God has given me?

*Lord, show me who I am to comfort and encourage today. And how — a phone call, an email, a card, an invitation≈*

## SATURDAY

**He gave thanks and broke the loaves. Then he gave them ...**

*Mark 6:41 (NIV)*

**Jesus took bread, and when he had given thanks, he broke it and gave it ...**

*Mark 14:22 (NIV)*

Jesus broke the bread several times – to feed 4,000, 5,000, the disciples at the last supper, in the home of the two who walked to Emmaus. Each time Jesus took the bread, he did the same thing – he broke it, then he gave thanks, and then he gave it.

And each time, out of the brokenness, there was a blessing as a miracle occurred. Feeding crowds, blessing the disciples, enduring the cross, blessing us; blessings out of thanksgiving. Even as he stood at the grave of his friend Lazarus, weeping openly, Jesus gave thanks (John 11:41).

*I have been broken by this bereavement. Heartbroken. Can I learn to give thanks in and through the breaking, and allow you, Lord Jesus, to bring a blessing through it? How can I learn that my broken dream is like an open door to another, maybe an even better dream, which can only come through my brokenness?*

I'll keep a list of the blessings, of the gifts, that Jesus gives me – even in my brokenness. I want to notice these things, however small – the smell of fresh coffee, the feel of an orange, a beautiful sky, my home.

*Here I go, Lord. Small things I've been blessed with recently. I'll do it again tomorrow, too.*

*Thank you for:*

*1*

*2*

*3*

# Reflections

Some photos, verses, poems and writings.
These are for you to dip into, look at, meditate
or simply enjoy as healing to your soul.

This deep, heart-searing loss has been strange and hard and disconcerting. I'm on the long journey of grief and the different emotions of that journey come and go, change and fluctuate.

The journey hasn't ended – maybe never will end. It's part of my life journey now, part of who I am.

*I take hold of God's promises.*

*I give thanks for having had this love in my life and for knowing such amazing love, given and received between us.*

*I give thanks that love never dies.*

# OAKS OF RIGHTEOUSNESS

The promise of Jesus:

**The Spirit of the Sovereign Lord is on me,**
**because the Lord has anointed me**
**to proclaim good news to the poor.**
**He has sent me to bind up the broken-hearted,**
**to proclaim freedom for the captives**
**and release from darkness for the prisoners,**
**to proclaim the year of the Lord's favour**
**and the day of vengeance of our God,**
**to comfort all who mourn,**
**and provide for those who grieve in Zion –**
**to bestow on them a crown of beauty**
**instead of ashes,**
**the oil of joy**
**instead of mourning,**
**and a garment of praise**
**instead of a spirit of despair.**
**They will be called oaks of righteousness,**
**a planting of the Lord**
**for the display of his splendour.**

*Isaiah 66:1-3 (NIV)*

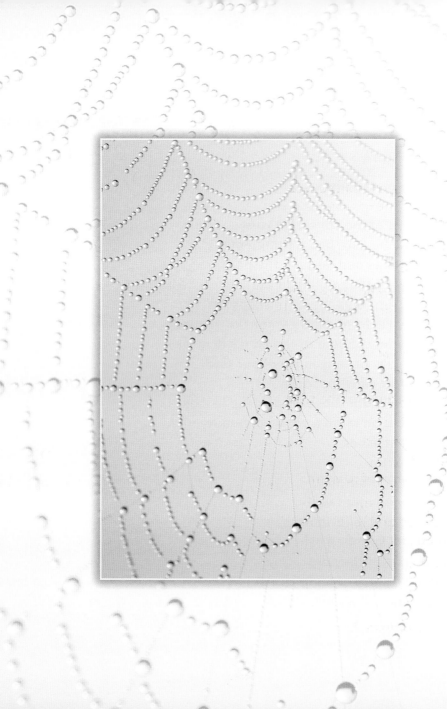

# THE GOSSAMER WEB

This gossamer of the web
reminds me of peace.

Fragile
Vulnerable
Easily torn apart.

This gossamer of the web
reminds me of peace.

Strong
Renewable
Resilient.

This gossamer of the web
reminds me of me.

Fragile yet strong
Vulnerable yet renewable
Torn apart yet resilient.

My peace is often broken and torn
restored and renewed
when I let God do it

My peace is renewed in God's love
Ultimately indestructible
A refraction of his love.

*P.J. Swithinbank*

# THE PROMISE OF PEACE
## Given by Jesus

*John 14:25-27*

The Friend, the Holy Spirit whom the Father will send at my request, will make everything plain to you. He will remind you of all the things I have told you. I'm leaving you well and whole. That's my parting gift to you. Peace. I don't leave you the way you're used to being left – feeling abandoned, bereft. So don't be upset. Don't be distraught.

*(MSG)*

I leave the gift of peace with you – my peace. Not the kind of fragile peace given by the world, but my perfect peace. Don't yield to fear or be troubled in your hearts – instead, be courageous!

*v. 27 (TPT)*

I am leaving you with a gift – peace of mind and heart. And the peace I give is a gift the world cannot give. So don't be troubled or afraid.

*v. 27 (NLT)*

# TIME FOR SOMETHING NEW

Time. Time for a new thing. The promise is there. I'm doing a new thing for you, says God. Don't you see it?

> *Forget the former things; do not dwell on the past.* **See, I am doing a new thing!** *Now it springs up; do you not perceive it? I am making a way in the wilderness and streams in the wasteland.*
>
> *Isaiah 43:18-19 (NIV)[21]*

God says, CHANGE YOUR FOCUS! STOP LOOKING BEHIND! START LOOKING AHEAD!

Our God is doing a new thing. Because the past won't sustain us. God says, 'Forget the former things . . . I am doing a new thing!'

Remember the children of Israel, and the stories in the Old Testament of how they wandered in the desert for forty years, and how they came to the Promised Land? They saw many victories.

Leaving Egypt. Entering the land of Canaan. Fighting off prospective conquerors. Disasters and detours and deaths. And also triumphs and conquests and seeing God provide miracles. But the past was doing nothing for them in the present. They needed a new work, a new miracle, a new victory.

So the question isn't: 'What has God done?' There's no doubt about that! The question must be: 'What new thing is God doing right now?'

The children of Israel had a choice to make. They were in exile, looking back at former glories. And looking back wasn't helping. Yet all they could see in the present was problems, and their own powerlessness. They didn't like where they were at the moment, and yet they didn't seem to trust **God** to change things for them, nor to want to be open to the possibilities he had in mind for them.

There is a choice:

They can continue as they are, nostalgic for what has been, yet not happy in the present, not trusting the Lord.

Or they can focus on what God wants to do in their lives. And God wants to do a new thing.

*Can I see possibilities if God is in charge of this new thing? In spite of, or maybe because of, my grief?*

The summer is the end of my year of mourning. I am returning – to the memories, to the first anniversary of The Day, to the return of what must become normal-but-without-her.

Can I see possibilities if God is in charge of this new thing, this new life, this new beginning which is now starting? Claim the new thing HE is doing for me? In me? Through me?

Returning – to a new thing. It's time. Time to return to God and to the new thing he is doing.

*O gracious and holy Father, give us wisdom to perceive you, diligence to seek you, patience to wait for you, eyes to behold you, a heart to meditate upon you, and a life to proclaim you; through the power of the Spirit of Jesus Christ our Lord.[22]*

# ONE THING

One thing I'm asking the Lord, this is what I'm wanting:
to be in his presence every single day of my life,
gazing on his beauty, making sure I'm worshipping him in a
sacred space.

Because in these days of trouble
he *will* keep me safe.
When I stay with the Lord
I will be calmed and renewed.
His power *will* strengthen me,
his love *will* bring me joy again,
his mercy will give me new life.
And the Lord *will* give me peace.

*P.J. Swithinbank – based on Psalm 27*

# WHY ME?

## questions to ask God

Why have you allowed this to happen to me, God? Why did you have to take ___ ? Have I been so bad that I deserve this sorrow and heartache? If you're a God of love, how can you let this awful death and the resulting grief overwhelm me? Where are you, God?

And why are some people allowed to live to an old age – is it because you're rewarding them or their families in some way? What have they done, or not done, to be allowed that joy?

Job's friends thought along these lines. The psalmists often say similar things and get very angry at God for letting bad things happen. But God furiously rejected the theology of Job's friends who tried to explain away all the terrible suffering Job was experiencing. The world is too deeply broken for an easy explanation. Yet God invites our questions, and there are many occasions in the Bible when people question him and shout at him and are angry at what has happened. God is big enough to take it!

The Bible never promises us an easy life – it does to start with, in the Garden of Eden, but then humanity turned away from God, sin entered the world, and part of the result is that sorrow and suffering entered the world too. The New Testament rejects the idea of suffering being a punishment sent by God to those who do bad things. Instead, it points to a God of love, who because of the enormous love he has for us, came to live among us and to be one with us and suffer with and for us. The idea of a God who punishes us doesn't ring true when there is so much in the Bible about his 'unfailing love'[23] for us, his compassion, his delight in us.

While we don't really know or understand why God allows the suffering to continue, we do know that it isn't because he doesn't love us, it isn't because he doesn't care. In fact, he cares so very much that he showed his commitment to our ultimate happiness and to mending our brokenness that he came to be a part of it. Because of that, he's promised that one day, all the sorrow and suffering will end, and he himself will wipe away the tears from our eyes.[24]

Maybe my 'why' questions show that I am still the centre of my own agenda, not allowing God to be the centre. Am I saying that he can be sovereign in everything except this?

Maybe it's enough to know that when we see him face to face, all the questions will be answered or be irrelevant.

In the meantime, we're too small, too limited, to understand the whys and the reasons. But not to grasp how vast and unlimited is his love for us. For me, for you. Even in this grief.

**I pray that out of his glorious riches he may strengthen you with power through his Spirit in your inner being, so that Christ may dwell in your hearts through faith. And I pray that you, being rooted and established in love, may have power, together with all the Lord's holy people, to grasp how wide and long and high and deep is the love of Christ, and to know this love that surpasses knowledge – that you may be filled to the measure of all the fullness of God.**

**Now to him who is able to do immeasurably more than all we ask or imagine, according to his power that is at work within us, to him be glory in the church and in Christ Jesus throughout all generations, for ever and ever! Amen.**

*Ephesians 3:16-21 (NIV)*

# AN INVITATION

Into my grieving
I weave
the strength of the Father.
Into my grieving
I weave
the compassion of the Son.
Into my grieving
I weave
the comfort of the Spirit
Into my grieving
I receive
the presence of the Three in One.

Into my anger
I invite
the patience of the Father.
Into my numbness
I invite
the healing of the Son.

Into my confusion
I invite
the wisdom of the Spirit.
And we shall grieve together,
I, in community
with the Three in One.[25]

# THE FELLOWSHIP OF THE MAT

'Mourn with those who mourn' wrote St Paul to the Roman Christians (Romans 12:15, NIV). He didn't say to give them lots of good advice, or to tell them it will end, or point out that others have it worse. He said very simply to mourn *with* them. Maybe that's the gift of presence, just *being* with someone in their grief, with little need for words. Job's friends did that with him – for seven whole days they were with him, sitting alongside him and sharing his suffering. Their words were rubbish, but their presence was a gift.

I need good friends to sit with me. Not to say anything and not to touch me. Words are confusing; hugs rub me raw. We can sit together, friends and I, with no need for words. I don't mind if they bring their knitting or their notebook. I don't want them to say much – and they can pray silently, thank you. But their support of presence is immense. They can pass the tissues.

And they can bring me to Jesus. I don't want to hear their prayers, because I can't pray and I don't know what to say and I can't bear too many words right now. I feel cut off from everyone, but especially from God, who seems to have left me in silence.

It will take four of them – one for each corner of my mat. They can carry me on my mat, lower me through the roof and place me at the feet of Jesus for him to do whatever he knows is best for me right now.

It's the fellowship of the mat. It's the blessing of community. It shows they love and care for me.

One day, I'll be carrying someone else's mat. But for now, I'm carried to the feet of Jesus by my dear friends. All I have to do is lie there.

> **They went up to the roof and took off some tiles. Then they lowered the sick man on his mat down into the crowd, right in front of Jesus.**
>
> *Luke 5:19 (NLT)*

# LEARNING TO LIVE WITHOUT

This is how it is, this learning to live again; this living with the sorrow and without-ness. Another lingering look back, not wanting to forget.

I shall not forget.

Yet there comes a time to move on, a time to learn to live again. To learn to live without. To live with it, my grief and sorrow; that emptiness which once she filled. My memories. Her love.

For love does not die. I love. She loves still. But not here. And so the space which once was her filling and her loving is my without-ness. I do not want the space to be filled with other people, other things and so I must, I need, to learn to live with it. From here until.

**Finally, be strong in the Lord and in his mighty power.**

*Ephesians 6:10 (NIV)*

Not the finally as we often think of finally – in our terminology that means 'I've got to the end at last.' Like a long sermon. No, for I shall not get to the end of my without-ness. But 'from now on, from now until the end.' From now on it will be like this. She will be missed and at times the without-ness will recede. Then it will crash back and overwhelm. This is how it is to be. Without-ness does not pass; it is not some passing whim. It is here to stay.

**But from now on, from now until the end, there can be strength 'in the Lord and in his mighty power.'**

**He does not pass and there is no without-ness with him.**

*Now may the Lord Jesus Christ and our Father God, who loved us and in his wonderful grace gave us eternal comfort and a beautiful hope that cannot fail,* encourage your hearts[26] *and inspire you with strength to always do and speak what is good and beautiful in his eyes.*

*2 Thessalonians 2:16-17 (TPT)*

# SNOWDROPS

There will be snowdrops again. There *will* be snowdrops again. I have to believe it. One day soon, the tiny tips will push through, struggling, light-seeking, upward-bound. First, there will be snow. Frost and freeze. Rain. Anything the elements can throw on a winter's day. A test of patience, hope, belief. But for now, the bulb lies cold, deeply hidden, dormant.

So lies my soul.

A corpse, buried in winter snow. Buried within my cold, cold body. Iced from within. I can see it from above, the rectangle of transparent ice surrounding all that is me.

It is hard to hear you through the ice. Impossible to reach out, touch you, feel your well-meant hug. This ice is brittle, sharp, so-very-cold. It forms a barrier.

Maybe that is my protection, for should the thaw come too soon I would feel too much.

So, I will believe that snowdrops will come again. And one day, one day, my snowdrop soul will grow again a tiny tip of life.

**For as [surely as] the earth brings forth its shoots, and as a garden causes what is sown in it to spring forth, so [surely] the Lord God will cause rightness and justice and praise to spring forth before all the nations [through the self-fulfilling power of His word].**

*Isaiah 61:11 (AMP Classic Edition)*

*A snowdrop is a bulb with a little hanging white, or green and white, flower which emerges in the cold of a January winter. But in Russian slang, 'snowdrop' can also refer to a corpse that has been buried in the snow and only appears when the thaws come.*

# BETWEEN WALLS

I found myself between Cotswold walls today.

I'd walked a mile or three, enjoyed the views and the warm caress of the late summer sun. Found a place I didn't know. Peered into old churches ringing with centuries of worship and liturgy and people. Imagined ancestors kneeling with toil-worn fingers and rheumaticky knees. Imagined them listening to the chants and the anthems. Imagined them slouching on the ancient pews, kept awake by fear of the wardens' poking poles. Imagined their prayers and cares, their dependence on God. And heard their silence.

I walked in the sun again, followed the lane as it wound through the trees, past the grand Manor House and the small thatched cottage. Smelled the last of the summer red roses, ran my fingers through the rosemary. And found myself between Cotswold walls. Higher than my head, topped with apple trees weighed down with the promise of harvest. The sun unable to compete with the height of the walls; I was shadowed.

Shadowed – and conscious of the heavy, heady silence. Sheltered. Away from reality. Away from the sunshine. Away from the views I was enjoying. The walls kept pace with the path. Or the path followed the walls. A narrow road. A dark road. A road of silence. Beyond: sunshine. Views. But here, for me, for now: Narrow. Dark. Silent.

And it was the parable of the past twenty-four months: two years of mourning. The years of narrow and dark and silent. Cut off from the land of the living. From the warmth and the sunshine. From the laughter. From the outward view. Confined to walk this path, hearing no one, seeing nothing, on and on.

And I knew that One had walked this way before me. Cut off from the land of living. Confined to silence and darkness. Narrowed. Broken. For me. And for you.

I trudged on. Glimpses of sunshine broke through. Glimpses of a vista, hints of spaces. I came to the chestnut tree and saw the horizon. And my eyes were open and my ears could hear and once again I was in the world around me.

And this is how it is. For him, the narrow, the dark, the silence of the tomb. And then the bursting forth. I greet the sunshine. The view. And know that it is his power at work in me to enable me to burst forth too. Slowly. Carefully. But it's happening. He's doing it.

# THE LAST BATTLE

'The term is over; the holidays have begun. The dream is ended: this is the morning.'

And as He spoke, He no longer looked to them like a lion; but the things that began to happen after that were so great and beautiful that I cannot write them.

And for us, this is the end of all the stories, and we can most truly say that they all lived happily ever after. But for them it was only the beginning of the real story.

All their life in this world and all their adventures in Narnia had only been the cover and the title page; now at last they were beginning Chapter One of the Great Story which no one on earth has ever read: which goes on forever; in which every chapter is better than the one before.

*C.S. Lewis,* The Last Battle[27]

I heard a loud shout from the throne, saying, 'Look, God's home is now among his people! He will live with them, and they will be his people. God himself will be with them.

He will wipe every tear from their eyes, and there will be no more death or sorrow or crying or pain. All these things are gone forever.' And the one sitting on the throne said, 'Look, I am making everything new!'

*And then he said to me, 'Write this down, for what I tell you is trustworthy and true.' And he also said, 'It is finished! I am the Alpha and the Omega – the Beginning and the End. To all who are thirsty I will give freely from the springs of the water of life.*

*All who are victorious will inherit all these blessings, and I will be their God, and they will be my children.'*

*Revelation 21:3-7 (NLT)*

# ACKNOWLEDGEMENTS

Thank you – to those who walked with me through my grief and through ensuing traumas.

Thank you to my dear friends, Angela and John, Margaret and Peter, Moyne and Phil, Sue and Tim. You have each been amazing and your love and prayers and support have kept me upright on more than one occasion. You are very special people in my life!

Thank you to my counsellors and therapists, Sally Worthington-Davies and Marilyn Tew, who have been patient and understanding and supplied never-ending tissues and coffee and listening ears. And great God-given wisdom.

Thank you to those who very kindly read the typescript and gave me huge encouragement, good ideas – and made me take out one or two lengthy paragraphs! Amy Boucher Pye, Kathryn Price, Jane Brocklehurst, Claire Musters: thank you for your sharp eyes and writerly advice.

Thank you to my publishers, Malcolm Down and Sarah Grace, for believing this new venture could work! And Sarah, thank you for your wise coaching. Thanks as well to Sheila Jacobs, my excellent editor, whose attention to detail has made a big difference.

Thank you to the Revd Canon Debbie Dewes, who has gifted us the glorious photos for this book. What a gift! They are stunning and I am very grateful. (Debbie retains the copyright.)

Thank you to my family. The biggest thanks to Robin and Rachel, Harriet and Stephen, Victoria and Gene, for your love, support and never-failing understanding. And for giving me such fabulous grandchildren.

And to my biggest support – thank you is almost too small, for all my gratitude and love for my husband, Kim, for his belief in me, his encouragement, his ability to sort out recalcitrant computers; and especially, of course, his love and support for me in my grief. I hope I never have to use this book in grieving for him, as I'd like to go together into the new best chapter of our lives, the new morning of eternity.

***SOLI DEO GLORIA***

# FURTHER HELP

Bereavement is a time when we often need the help and support of others. Friends are good. People who understand and have expert help are also very good! I am very grateful to the counsellor and the spiritual director who each walked with me though my grief and helped me to come to terms with my loss. I would certainly recommend talking with both a counsellor and a spiritual director.[28]

Ask people for recommendations. You can also google local counsellors in your locality – most will offer grief counselling, and some will be specialists in this area and will say so on their websites.

Or you could look at the following:

**Association of Christian Counsellors (ACC)**
www.acc-uk.org

**Cruse Bereavement Care**
www.cruse.org.uk

**Sarah Grace, psychotherapist/counsellor**
www.sarahmgrace.co.uk
email: grace4counselling@gmail.com

**Penelope Swithinbank, spiritual director**
https://penelopeswithinbank.com/spiritual-direction

**Swift Counselling and psychotherapy**
http://www.swift-counselling.co.uk

# NOTES

[1] See Isaiah 9:6.

[2] KJV.

[3] For example, see John 14:27, NIV.

[4] Various versions.

[5] Revelation 21:6, various versions.

[6] Classic Edition.

[7] Book of Common Prayer 1662, copyright Cambridge University Press.

[8] See Darby, KJV.

[9] Philippians 4:7 from the RSV.

[10] Adam Clarke's Commentary on the Bible (Grand Rapids, MI: Baker Publishing Group, 1983).

[11] Luke 8:25.

[12] https://www.missionstclare.com/english/canticle/9.html (accessed 11.12.20).

[13] Corrie Ten Boom Quotes. BrainyQuote.com, BrainyMedia Inc, 2021. https://www.brainyquote.com/quotes/corrie_ten_boom_381184 (accessed 18.1.21).

[14] Seventeenth-century clergyman and poet.

[15] Michael Card, John Thompson, 'El Shaddai'. Produced by Brown Bannister.

[16] The Geneva Bible of 1587.

[17] See TPT.

18  Book of Common Prayer 1662, copyright Cambridge University Press.

19  I am aware that Paul is writing to the Corinthians about money and giving, but it seems to me that the principles apply to every aspect of our lives.

20  Such as KJV.

21  Emphasis mine.

22  A Prayer of St Benedict, https://www.catholicteacher.com/prayer-from-st-benedict/july-11/ (accessed 11.12.20).

23  For example, see Psalms (NIV).

24  See Revelation 7:17.

25  Quoted in the prayers online by St Bartholomew's Episcopal Church, Yarmouth, ME, https://stbyarmouth.files.wordpress.com/2020/10/pastoral-care-booklet-for-website.pdf (accessed 18.1.21).

26  The Bible version tells us that 'The Aramaic can be translated: "He will comfort your hearts . . ."' See https://www.biblegateway.com/passage/?search=2+thessalonians+2%3A16-17&version=TPT (accessed 11.12.20). Emphasis mine.

27  THE LAST BATTLE by C.S. Lewis copyright © C.S. Lewis Pte. Ltd. 1956 Extract reprinted by permission.

28  Spiritual directors are people who have trained to help others in their spiritual journey, by listening, praying, guiding; and by helping them grow in their faith.